T0353332

THE OBERON BOOK OF
MODERN MONOLOGUES FOR MEN
VOLUME 2

THE OBERON BOOK OF MODERN MONOLOGUES FOR MEN

Chosen and Edited by Catherine Weate

OBERON BOOKS
LONDON
www.oberonbooks.com

First published in 2013 by Oberon Books Ltd
521 Caledonian Road, London N7 9RH
Tel: +44 (0) 20 7607 3637 / Fax: +44 (0) 20 7607 3629
e-mail: info@oberonbooks.com
www.oberonbooks.com

Compilation copyright © Catherine Weate, 2013

Reprinted in 2013, 2014, 2016

Catherine Weate is hereby identified as author of this compilation
of extracts of plays in accordance with section 77 of the Copyright,
Designs and Patents Act 1988. The author has asserted her moral rights.

The contributors are hereby identified as authors of their contributions
in accordance with section 77 of the Copyright, Designs and Patents
Act 1988. The authors have asserted their moral rights.

All rights whatsoever in these extracts are strictly reserved and
application for performance, other than in an audition context,
should be made before commencement of rehearsal to the authors'
agents. No performance may be given unless a licence has been obtained,
and no alterations may be made in the title or the text of the play
without the author's prior written consent.

You may not copy, store, distribute, transmit, reproduce or otherwise
make available this publication (or any part of it) in any form, or
binding or by any means (print, electronic, digital, optical, mechanical,
photocopying, recording or otherwise), without the prior written
permission of the publisher. Any person who does any unauthorized act
in relation to this publication may be liable to criminal prosecution and
civil claims for damages.

A catalogue record for this book is available from the British Library.

PB ISBN: 9781849434362
E ISBN: 9781849436052

Cover image © Imagesource.com

Visit www.oberonbooks.com to read more about all our books and to
buy them. You will also find features, author interviews and news of any
author events, and you can sign up for e-newsletters so that you're always
first to hear about our new releases.

Catherine Weate is a freelance voice and dialect coach. She has worked in theatre, film, television, radio, education, commerce, law and politics across England, Australia, Hong Kong, Africa and India. Her former roles include: Head of Voice at Rose Bruford College, Head of Voice and Vice Principal at the Academy of Live and Recorded Arts and Head of Examinations at LAMDA. Catherine's other titles published by Oberon Books are: *Modern Voice: Working with Actors on Contemporary Text, Classic Voice: Working with Actors on Vocal Style, The Oberon Book of Modern Monologues for Women 1, The Oberon Book of Modern Monologues for Men 1, The Oberon Book of Modern Monologues for Women 2,* and *The Oberon Book of Modern Duologues.*

INTRODUCTION

Monologues are an essential part of every actor's toolkit. Why? Because actors are required to perform monologues regularly throughout their career: in particular, preparing for drama school entry, showcasing skills for agents or auditioning for a professional role. But what actually is a monologue? And how do you go about choosing the right one for you?

A monologue is nothing more than a speech by a single character in a play or screenplay. Sometimes the character might speak their thoughts aloud to themselves, sometimes they might engage in a lengthy speech to another character and sometimes they will directly address the audience, breaking down the 'fourth wall'.

Choosing a monologue, however, is a delicate task. The only givens are that the character should be close to your age (or in your playing range) and the text should be sufficiently interesting (on its own without the rest of the play) to hold the attention of an audience. Most importantly, it must speak to you, resonate with your inner emotions, affect your senses, make you laugh or cry and draw you into a world that you want to hear more about. But don't forget that if you are using the monologue in a professional audition then it must resemble the job in some way, through genre, period, culture and/or character (including accent).

Some coaches have particular 'rules' for choosing a monologue. Let me assure you that there is no 'right' or 'wrong'. Trust your inner instincts when making your choice, as long as the piece is appropriate for the context in which it is to be performed. There are coaches who advise avoiding monologues that are: physically still, tell a story about the past, directly address the audience or use vulgarity. None of these rules apply (unless stipulated by an audition panel or casting agent). Controversial content is tricky to avoid in contemporary theatre texts (after all, modern plays often seek to mirror the real world), and a well-written character-driven story spoken directly to an audience can be riveting.

Other coaches advise actors to avoid monologue books; however, they can be a terrifically useful tool and a great starting point. Better than being overwhelmed by rows of plays in bookshops or libraries. They only work though if you read the full play text from which your monologue has been drawn. Picking a piece from a book and performing it without further reading or research is madness and, ultimately, your character study will be superficial and incomplete. Read the play to understand the journey/trajectory of plot, character, relationship and situation. If possible, try to see the play in performance to understand how the monologue (and therefore the character) works in context.

This monologue book showcases the writing from authors published by Oberon Books (following on from the first volume of *The Oberon Book of Modern Monologues for Men*, published in 2008). There are a diverse range of quirky and memorable characters that cross cultural and historical boundaries. Yes, some of them tell stories, many directly address the audience and, being contemporary plays, there is quite a bit of controversial material. As there should be.

The pieces have been organised into age-specific groups: 'teens', 'twenties', 'thirties' and 'forties plus'. However, there is the occasional character that crosses these boundaries so do spend some time reading outside of your age-related box, just in case (particularly true of text in the 'twenties' and 'thirties' sections). The boundaries are simply there to provide you with a starting point.

Monologue length varies widely depending on the material: the concise and contained to the weighty and protracted. Don't be afraid of adapting them to your needs, particularly when many auditions stipulate time frames for performance. In a few cases I have cut texts to maintain flow and sense. This is indicated by '…' on a line all of its own, between paragraphs.

If you require any further information or advice on these books (all feedback is welcome) or in choosing/performing a monologue then please contact me through my website (www. catherineweate.com) or on twitter (@voicesupport). In the meantime, happy reading.

Catherine Weate

CONTENTS

PART THREE: THIRTIES

PART FOUR: FORTIES PLUS

PART ONE: TEENS

SHADOWMOUTH
by Meredith Oakes

Shadowmouth *was first performed at the Crucible Theatre in Sheffield on 8 June 2006.*

A fifteen-year-old BOY is thrown out of home by his mother and taken in by a lonely middle-aged man. He watches the BOY from a distance, filled with desire. But the BOY is in a dark depression and cannot be saved. He tries to lose himself in the seediness of city nightlife and assorted relationships but nothing helps and he heads for destruction.

BOY

One night, I reached the centre of town

It was like discovering a whole unknown tribe

People awake at night

Like me

Going about their business in the middle of the night as if it were the most ordinary thing in the world

While everyone I knew was asleep in bed

All the rules were turned upside-down

Drink, drugs, visions and sex were everyone's serious business

While the business buildings, the government offices, the gallery, the museum, slept like dark forgotten giants

There were lit up places floating like boats on the city darkness, and in them were pirates and ruffians, girls with smudged eyes and bare flesh, drinkers staring down into wells of alcohol, fat hairy men in black leather, women in bowler hats, people with cigarette holders and rings on their fingers

It was like seeing through the skin of the city down into where it had always been like this, century upon century

It was like seeing the hidden life now visible and glowing, everyone decked out as the self of their dreams

I didn't know who I might see lining up to the bar

Christopher Marlowe

The Queen of Sheba

I'd never seen a floor with so much dirt on it, the dirt of centuries

Fag-ends in drifts

Grit piling up against the skirting boards

And people slopping drinks as they passed, calling to each other across the noise

The air was at saturation point with alcohol, smoke and sweat

The place felt ready to burst into flame

It was here

Whatever would make me real

I was in the room with the animal

I could see its rolling eye, its velvet mouth, its foam-flecked shoulder, its huge flank

I could feel the heavy stumbling of its hooves in the straw

I loved it

THE LOSS OF ALL THINGS
by *Chris Goode*

from *SIXTY-SIX BOOKS: 21ˢᵗ-Century Writers
Speak to the King James Bible*

Sixty-Six Books: 21st-Century Writers Speak to the King
James Bible *was first performed at the Bush Theatre in London
on 10 October 2011. On 14 and 28 October, the sixty-six
texts were performed back-to-back in an all-night vigil at
the Bush. On 28 October they were performed complete at
Westminster Abbey.*

Sixty-Six Books is a celebration of the 400ᵗʰ anniversary of
the King James Version of the Bible. Sixty-six writers were
commissioned to interpret a book from the KJV for the
twenty-first century. They include playwrights, poets, novelists
and songwriters differing in gender, age, ethnicity, sexual
orientation and faith. *The Loss of All Things* is Chris Goode's
response to the 'Philippians'. TIM is a thirteen-year-old boy
in Year 9. His best friend is Paul, who is thinking about killing
himself. Instead, TIM wants to keep Paul alive in a room at the
back of the cellar to practise his experiments on, just like he did
with the family dog.

TIM

…when I was younger, couple of years ago, and my mum was starting to get ill, my mum and my dad got me a dog. I'd wanted a dog for ages and they said I could have a dog as long as it was me that took care of it and everything. It was called Shreds. It was a lab retriever. Friendly. Good personality. There were two of them, Shreds and Patches. And they got split up because the owner couldn't cope any more. She had a, um…nervous breakdown.

And it was fine, for a while, having Shreds around, and then I started thinking about how it would be interesting to have a dog that was like a ghost or something. Like it would still follow you around but it wouldn't quite be alive exactly. So I got this notebook, you know, and I started doing drawings of ghost dogs and weird sort of not-quite dogs and dogs that were made out of rubbish and stuff.

And I drew this one that was like a skeleton dog. But it still worked. You could see its heart or whatever. And I started to think, you know, how much of a dog could you actually get rid of and it would still work.

I was looking it up on the internet and stuff. Like, what's like actually inside a dog?

And there were pictures from like scientific experiments and stuff where there's only, there's not quite a whole dog. It's like, some of it's been cut away. Like when you've started eating a chicken and it's in the fridge the next day.

So I did sketches of these like science dogs. And you could see their skulls or whatever. Their ribs with a heart. Shaped like a proper heart.

Anyway.

It was quite lucky that my mum started getting really ill, in a way, because no one was thinking about Shreds. So I could just... No one was like, where's Shreds?

And then I read this thing about where you take the bark out. Like you can actually debark them, surgically. Or not necessarily exactly surgically exactly. But so then it's just... Because it's easier after that.

But I wouldn't do that to you. Necessarily.

DESERT BOY
by Mojisola Adebayo
from *Mojisola Adebayo: Plays One*

Desert Boy *was commissioned and produced by NITRO and the Albany Theatre and premiered at the Albany in London, on 28 April 2010.*

Junior Watson, aka SOLDIER BOY, is sixteen years old and part of black South London gang culture. As he bleeds from a knife wound on Deptford beach, a strange traveller from the past appears: Desert Man from Mali. He takes SOLDIER BOY on a journey through black colonial history to discover his past and, ultimately, himself. Time travel is juxtaposed with the events in SOLDIER BOY's life that led to Deptford beach: in this scene, we find him alone, dispossessed and frightened on a train. Later we discover that his wound was self-inflicted: 'I'm scared, people are scared of me' and 'they're not gonna get me. Not my crew, a dog or next gang, not the police or a bunch of racists. I'll do it myself.'

SOLDIER BOY

The last stop South. I'm going anywhere from Lewisham, anywhere from this life. People **push past** and steal my backwards seat. A college kid sits there **drawing lines** on a pad **random**. The other one's taken by a banker biting her lip, **tap tapping** on her blackberry. Why they wanna name a phone after a fruit? Why can't they call things what they are? **Tap tap, scritch scraaatch.** The rest is **tourists**. It's like the whole carriage is **tormenting** me. They all watch me but **pretend not to see me**, nervously, like when someone owes you money. I clock them **aaaaall** out of the corner of my hoody. I slump on a sideways seat and **stare into space**.

...

And the doors of the train close me in. Where am I going to? Where am I going? Train pulls off **can't catch my** breath. Out **pop pops** the sweat. Head hot, feet cold. **Then swap.** Train speeds up, **switches tracks**. My heart tick tocks then **stops**. Come back. **Come back!** The beat's in my throat and I wanna throw up. I'm dizzy, **boiling hot**. And I **blink blink blink**. It's black. **Blink blink.** There's stars. **Blink** and suddenly a **black man** appears opposite and he's staring at me! **Why does he look so angry?** Does he know me? **Has General sent someone already? One of Jesus men? A ghost,** the boy from my dream? He looks like me, but **it can't be daddy.** Out of his hoody I see the whites of his **glaring eyes** and I'm terrified. **Split second** then I realise, I realise it's me, my reflection. I see what they all see. SOLDIER BOY *talking to his reflection.*

...

The train speeds **round a bend** and into Deptford Bridge.

…

And on steps the crew.

…

Savage lunges at me and I pull out my knife. I hear a **laugh, a deep loud laugh** then **screeeeeeeams**. A **rush of blood**, at last, I am released.

MRS REYNOLDS
AND THE RUFFIAN
by Gary Owen

*This play was first performed at Watford Palace Theatre
on 15 April 2010.*

Mrs Reynolds and the Ruffian is set 'somewhere in present-day Britain'. Mrs Reynolds' garden has been vandalised by a troubled youth, JAY. Social services organise a truce and stipulate that JAY must fix the damage he has caused. Despite their differences, a strong bond forms between JAY and Mrs Reynolds. In a rare moment, he confides in her about his early life.

JAY

When I was little, all I remember is

My mum, always sick

And me worrying about her all the time.

She had doctors coming every day

To give her medicine.

Except it wasn't medicine.

And the men weren't really doctors.

And sometimes she didn't have money.

So she'd pay for 'her medicine' in other ways.

There was this one bloke

She called him Holliman

I walked into the lounge one day

Found mum on her knees, in front of him.

I didn't know what it meant.

After that, mum put a lock on my door

On the outside.

They used to lock me in – for my own sake.

Stop me seeing things I shouldn't.

But they'd get so wasted, they'd forget I was there.

One time I had to shit in the corner of my room.

I couldn't help myself.

I was seven. It was hurting my belly. Holliman

Rubbed my nose in it.

Held my face down

And rubbed my nose in my own shit.

Said that would teach me.

He would bring men round,

Let them use my mum.

Before they locked me in, mum

Would give me a pot noodle

And the kettle, so I could feed myself.

I would eat every mouthful and think –

See? My mum loves me, really.

One time I heard her screaming.

I kicked the door till the lock gave way

Holliman was standing over her, his foot

On her throat.

I stabbed him in the leg with my penknife.

And she –

– she threw me out.

I was thirteen.

And I don't look to her for nothing these days.

I just thank her.

For everything she taught me.

For how strong she made me.

FIT
by Rikki Beadle-Blair

Fit was commissioned by Queer Up North and Stonewall and its first UK tour of schools began in September 2007. The original play was adapted into a film in 2010.

Focusing on the issues surrounding homophobic bullying, *Fit* follows a group of late teens who are part of a school dance group. JORDAN is 17, of African descent and a talented athlete/footballer. He's in love with his best friend Tegs (who turns out isn't gay, despite general opinion) but has been too afraid to tell him…until now. In this scene, JORDAN not only reveals his sexuality but also explains why he was kicked out of his last college.

JORDAN

When Lee spoke up. I should have said it. 'I'm gay too.'

…

'Cause its true. I should have stood up and said it – loud and proud and sod everyone else.

…

I got kicked out for fighting – like I told you.

…

I was in love.

…

With a lad called Melvin. He was lovely. Dead skinny, but lovely. He was out. He was proud. And they used to knock seven bells out of him. They used to spit on his back from the top of the stairs. They used to steal his stuff and piss on it and worse. And he was like you. He never cried. They did some right horrible things. Constantly. Just torturing him. And I used to let 'em. I used to watch. And I never said nothing. Til one day, he tried to kill hisself. Tried to hang hisself with his shirt in the changing rooms while the rest of us was playing football. I don't know why he chose the changing room. Yeah, I do. So we'd find him there. So we'd discover him. It was meant to be his final statement. But he didn't die. Just nearly. Ambulance came. Took him away. And people started laughing about it. Straight back to taking the piss. Someone found Melvin's bag – started to kick it about. And I snapped. I went mental. I broke this lad's cheekbone. I'm not sorry. He deserved it. I deserved it. I was another coward just like them. When I should have been brave like Melvin.

…

So you wanna kiss us or what?

DNA

by Dennis Kelly

DNA *was first performed in the Cottesloe Theatre of the National Theatre, London, on 16 February 2008.*

A group of teenagers bully, torture and kill (or so they think) one of their classmates, Adam. Their panic leads to a bold cover-up. MARK and Jan explain what happened to those in the group who weren't there. Apparently it started out as a joke with various degrees of torture and physical abuse. MARK's monologue outlines the final moments.

MARK

We went up the grille. You know, that shaft up there on the hill. Just a big hole really, hole with a grille over it, covering, just to see if he'd climb the fence, really and he did, and we thought, you know, he's climbed the fence which we didn't think he'd do so walk, you know, walk on the grille, Adam, walk on the, and he did, he's walked on, you know, wobbling and that but he's walking on the grille and we're all laughing and he's scared because if you slip, I mean it's just blackness under you, I mean it's only about fifteen foot wide so, but it might be hundreds of feet into blackness, I dunno, but he's doing it, he's walked on the grille. He's on the grille. He is.

And someone's pegged a stone at him.

Not to hit him, just for the laugh.

And you shoulda seen his face, I mean the fear, the, it was so, you had to laugh, the expression, the fear…

So we're all peggin them. Laughing. And his face, it's just making you laugh harder and harder, and they're getting nearer and nearer. And one hits his head. And the shock on his face is so…funny. And we're all just…

just…

really chucking these stones into him, really hard and laughing and he slips.

And he drops.

Into…

Into the er...

So he's...

So he's...

So he's –

BLACKBERRY TROUT FACE
by Laurence Wilson

This play was first performed at the Unity Theatre, Liverpool
on 29 September 2009.

Set in Liverpool, *Blackberry Trout Face* explores the lives of
three teenagers who are struggling to cope on their own. JAKEY
(18), Kerrie (15) and Cameron (13) have been abandoned by
their mother, a heroin addict who feeds her habit through
prostitution. JAKE, as the eldest, is expected to take charge.
Instead, he wants to run away and join the army to escape his
life in a street gang. He tries to explain why to his younger
sister and brother.

JAKEY

A couple of weeks ago.

...

We was out an about see. I was just like er...sittin off on a wall and a few of the little dickheads started happy slappin some prozzy. They was pushin her round and she come near enough for me to see her properly. *(Beat.)* It was her.

...

Mum.

...

Her nose was bleedin and she was dead scared, shakin...and she...she looked so...so small... She was...she was beggin them to stop.

...

She saw me and I thought she'd...but she...she didn't... She didn't say me name... She... She didn't want them to know she knew me... She didn't...didn't want them to know that she was...that she was me Mum.

...

None of them hadn't never seen me with her, so they didn't know who she was. They started eggin me to hit her. I grabbed hold of her. She was just...just lookin at me... She made me feel sick. I wanted to...wanted to smash her face in.

...

They was all shoutin, smack that bitch Jakey, smack that bitch. So I pulled my fist back. I wanted to hit her. I could see me knuckles smashin into her nose, I saw meself just hittin her and hittin her over and over until she had no face left. They was all like, what are yer waitin for Jakey? Smack the bitch. And then it just came out.

…

I said, this bitch is my Mum. They all started laughin. So I repeated it. This bitch is my Mum. They got it that time. She started cryin and everyone just stood there. I looked at her and I looked at them. If it had been anyone else they'd been slappin around, I'd have done nothing. Coz that's what it is out there.

Then I told her to go and she did. I watched her walk off all funny coz one of her heels had broke off. No one said nothin but I knew that was it for me. I don't want none of it no more. I've gotta go, and the army is me only way out.

…

Yer think yer can just leave a gang like that and walk round like yer was never a part of it? Yer think they'll have that? The things I know, the things I've seen. It doesn't work like that. It's lifetime membership. The only way to escape is to disappear, one way or the other. I've just had enough of it. I hate it. I've gotta get away from them.

…

Every day out there with them I'm... I'm becomin... Losin it... Another couple of months on, I might have done it. I might of joined in. Because she'd just be another victim like all the rest. *(Beat.)* I have to go.

WHAT FATIMA DID...
by Atiha Sen Gupta

This play was first performed at Hampstead Theatre in London on 22 October 2009.

Fatima is a British born Asian, who has embraced the wild life of a London teenager. However, on the eve of her 18th birthday, without warning, she starts wearing the hijab. Although we never see her in the play, we do see how her friends and family react to what she did. Her twin brother, MOHAMMAD, doesn't condone Fatima's actions, but he does try to explain to their mother what it's like to be Asian and living in contemporary English society.

MOHAMMED

(Snapping.) You don't know what it's like! Times have
changed! It's not about Paki this or Paki that. I understand
that. But it's not that. They don't even hate Asians anymore,
they hate us…specifically us…and I feel sick. Some days
I can barely go out on to the street, on the tube, to school
without feeling like my throat's gonna seize up. They look at
us…they know who we are and they hate us…the amount
of fucking times I've got on the train and people have moved
away from me…and I know exactly what's going on up here.
(MOHAMMED taps his head.) They're thinking that at least
if they're in the further part of the carriage, then when my
bomb goes off, they'll lose a leg or an arm – but not their
lives. I know they're not getting up to get off the train 'cos
I watch them… I fucking watch them. And they watch me
watching them. And they NEVER get off at the next stop.
Never. And you wanna know the worst thing? They give me
that pathetic fucking I'm-ever-so-polite English half-smile like
this *(MOHAMMED demonstrates this smile.)* before they
move away from me. *(Pause, breathing in heavily.)* When
you see a white person with a backpack on, everyone thinks
backpacker… But when you see an Asian with a backpack
on, you're only left with terrorist. And that's what I'm
saying. Why can't we all be backpackers? Give me an answer
and I'll be happy. I just want an answer. *(Beat.)* And even
though I would never have imagined Fatima in a million years
putting on the hijab before she did, I don't blame her and I
understand. I understand how she did it even though I don't
know *why*. *(Crying.)* I don't know why.

SHRADDHA
(Faith: You are what's in your heart)
by *Natasha Langridge*

Shraddha *was first performed at Soho Theatre, London, on*
29 October 2009.

The Romany Gypsies are about to be evicted from the building
site of the London Olympics. Understandably they are more
suspicious than usual of outsiders (gorgers). Pearl Penfold is
17 years old and has been promised in marriage to another
Romany community. However, she and JOE, a gorger from the
local council estate have fallen in love. In this scene, JOE tries
to appeal to Pearl's family and delivers the following speech
outside their trailer. Ultimately, JOE's appeals are fruitless and
the young lovers run away together.

JOE

I'm sorry to disturb yer... Mrs Penfold... Mr Penfold

Sound of dogs barking.

I had to come

Back

I had to

I know what yer said about what you'd do to me teeth
but
I've come to ask yer
to your face
Straight

Can I come in?

Will you come out?

I know what yer said before 'bout my knees
But if yer knew what was in me
Please
Give me a go to win your daughter's heart
I know I ain't rich
I know I ain't all the things I gotta be
But I can learn
If yer show me
Yer ways
Teach me how you do it
I never had no one to teach me
It ain't my fault I was born a gorger
I'll work harder than you even

I'll work and work and work
till I'm *it*
Please
Give me a go

Please answer me

I ain't goin' away

I can't
I was just dragging around in the dark before
No light
Anywhere

But in her

Brightness
Life like I never seen

Please
What can I do?

I gotta have it

Gets on his knees.

Her

Tell me an I'll do it

I'll do it

Please

He waits for a long time.
More and more dogs are barking.

PART TWO: TWENTIES

POSH

by Laura Wade

*This play was first performed at The Royal Court Jerwood
Theatre Downstairs in London on 9 April 2010.*[1]

The ten student members of Oxford University's elite Riot
Club are holding one of their famous dinners in a private room
at a gastropub. It's turning into a wild night but not exactly
as they planned. The prostitute has refused to service them
under the table and the pub owner has asked them to behave.
ALISTAIR RYLE, somewhere between 19 and 21 years of age,
is outraged.

---

[1] The text extract reprinted here is taken from the published edition of
the 2010 production. The text reprinted by Oberon Books for the West
End revival in 2012 contains revisions that Laura Wade made for this
production.

ALISTAIR

What a fucking. Knob-jockey.

…

I don't care if he hears me. I'm sorry, but what was *that*? What does he *think*? What does he think is happening here?

…

Does he think he's some kind of *lord* 'cause he's got a gastropub? What, thin beef and gay puddings for people who think 'cause they're eating orange fish it must be smoked salmon? 'Cause he can get 'patio', 'lavatory' and 'facilities' into one sentence, yeah?

…

Calling us 'Gentlemen' as if he had any idea, any *idea* of what the word means. God, the look on his face when I gave him that cash – Tom and Jerry pound signs in his eyes. Graciously letting us stay if we don't smoke or call a prozzer or make any noise – what is this, the fucking Quiet Carriage?

…

You know, checking we do want that many bottles ''cause it seems quite a lot for ten people'. Not this ten people, mate. But you know what, *we're not people*.

Cause *people* – people like him – you know, honest, decent hardworking people hell-bent on turning this country to fuck. He thinks he can have anything if he works hard enough. He also thinks Rugby League is a sport. He thinks his daughter's getting a useful education at Crapsville College or wherever she's – I mean this man keeps cheese in the fucking *fridge*.

...

'While you're under my roof you respect my rules'? I've got a new rule for you, mate, it's called survival of the fittest, it's called 'fuck you – we're the Riot Club'. Respect that. 'Can't have one rule for them and another rule for you' – why not? Seriously, why the fuck not? We're the fucking Riot Club. And we've hardly started, mate.

And *her*, people like her, the stuck up bitch, fucking skank – you're a prostitute, love, get on your knees. 'Not doing that, it's not in my job description', 'I'm a professional, I need a proper break' – even the hookers want paid holidays – 'Ring my line manager' – I'll wring your fucking neck if you're not careful. Where's your *imagination*? – we've got the finest sperm in the country in this room, she should be paying *us* to let her drink it.

...

And these people think *we're* twats. Are we going to sit here and take it, carry on taking it? Who the fuck are they, anyway? How did they get *everywhere*, how did they make everything so fucking second-rate?

Thinking they're cultured 'cause they read a big newspaper and eat asparagus and pretend not to be racist. Bursting a vein at the thought there's another floor their lift doesn't go up to, for all their *striving*, for all their making everything *accessible* and fucking mediocre. 'Isn't that shopping centre lovely?' It's not fucking lovely, it's just *new*. It's a fucking mirage for you to spend invisible money that isn't even yours and then blame it on me for being fucking born. 'You can't have that, that's not fair.' You know what's not fair? That we have to even listen to them. Thinking 'cause there's more of them, they're better when they're worth their weight in shit. Saying 'it's not about the money' on the in breath and 'give it give it give it' on the out, mixing up quantity and quality like it's a fucking cocktail I mean I am sick, I am sick to fucking death of *poor people*.

SPUR OF THE MOMENT
by Anya Reiss

This play was first performed at The Royal Court Jerwood Theatre Upstairs, London, on 14 July 2010.

DANIEL is a twenty-one-year-old student and rents a room in the home of twelve-year-old Delilah. Delilah's parents, Vicky and Nick, are too busy arguing to notice that their daughter has become infatuated with the lodger. DANIEL's precarious emotional state, exacerbated by a visit from his girlfriend, leads him to returning Delilah's affection. However, he hates himself and tries to put her off by confessing his faults.

DANIEL

I'm a pathetic loser. I'm a bad person. Really…you wouldn't believe how bad I am. I…I'm a…I used to lose my temper at home and hit my dad not even for real reasons just self-indulgence. Once left the dog food can open and my dog got hold of it cut his face up with the edge of the can and got stuck in it, blood all over the kitchen my parents were out so I just left him overnight. Spat at my old girlfriend in the face to make her leave me because I just didn't want to see her anymore, I'd just be mad at her whenever I saw her. No reason, she hadn't done anything. I lie all the time. Haven't done any of my essays for uni. I've cut myself before I don't even know why I just… I just did and Leonie thinks it was because of her but it wasn't and so she feels like she has to stay with me even though, even though she isn't the problem. She's the best person I've ever met and she loves me but I can't love her, I've tried I really am trying but she, she just, she's so fucking irritating….. I say I don't believe in God but I think I actually do, I just say it to be different… Can't afford your parent's rent. I…I… *(Running out of confessional steam.)* And for some reason I can't stop myself, just like your tourettes thing I keep thinking I don't care anymore 'so what' so I kiss you even though I feel sick and it's so wro…and… and… You don't love me so much now do you?

JAMES DEAN IS DEAD!
(LONG LIVE JAMES DEAN)

by Jackie Skarvellis

from *Hollywood Legends: 'Live' on Stage*

*This one-man play was first performed at Above the Stag
Theatre, London on 4 June 2009.*

The actor, JAMES DEAN, died in a fatal car crash in 1955
at the age of 24. He is best remembered for the films *East of
Eden, Rebel Without a Cause* and *Giant*, which made him into
a Hollywood star. In this one-man play, DEAN is resurrected
from the dead to talk about sex, love, acting, stardom and his
final days. He speaks directly to the audience. The following
monologue occurs just after he has explained how his supposed-
girlfriend, the Italian actress Pier Angeli, ended up marrying
somebody else.

JAMES DEAN

The loneliness – I scream inside my skin, inside my skull.
There's nowhere so lonely as the big city. Busy people, coming
and going. All of them, all day long, with their busy little
lives. 'We're busy doing nothing, but buzzing around like flies!'
Sweet fuck nothings. I try and keep myself busy too: I take
lessons in dancing with Eartha Kitt; I take classes – anything
to keep the void at bay. The city never sleeps and neither
do I. I haunt the bars, I hunt in the bars. You meet some
strange insomniacs like yourself, hag-ridden, hollow-eyed,
sleepwalkers in the twilight world, that in-between world.
Sometimes I fuck 'em, sometimes I send 'em home. Alien
encounters in the dead of night, but the neon is always bright,
relentless, even in the dead of night. I walk the dark side of
my inner soul. Close encounters of an intimate kind that mean
nothing. Sometimes, I watch two people fucking, I play the
voyeur. I don't do anything. It's all part of my training, I tell
myself, to break new ground with my acting technique. I tell
myself it's all good experience. *(Laughs.)* All sortsa people get
caught in my net: human detritus! Most of 'em I throw away
with the dawn, but it stops the loneliness…sometimes…

KURT AND SID
by Roy Smiles

Kurt and Sid *was produced by Surefire Theatrical Ltd and first performed at Trafalgar Studios on 9 September 2009.*

In 1994, Kurt Cobain, the frontman of Nirvana, is planning to kill himself. However, just as he's about to pull the trigger, SID VISCIOUS, Kurt's hero from the Sex Pistols appears in order to talk him out of it. Is he a ghost? Or is he a figment of Kurt's imagination? In this monologue, SID delivers the ultimate argument.

SID

Look – I wish I could tell you it's a beautiful world but it's not. You want me to believe in all things bright and beautiful? I can't. Like I said I don't believe in any of it. Sunsets, just some shit you can't touch over there: flowers, get in the way of the pavement; the birds in the sky, winged wankers that crap on my shoulder. Rainbows, I'm colour blind. My life's in black and white: all shades grey. Don't ask me to tell you how pretty the world is. I don't see the majesty of humanity: I just see the bastards who grind you down. I see a world with no redeeming features. No happiness. No joy. Don't ask for a pep talk. You've got the wrong coach. I bat for the other team. Nah, I can't do all that for-every-drop-of-rain-that-falls-a-flower-grows shit. All I can tell you is this: it matters, music; in the void, into the emotionless pit of people's lives. Most people only marry to fuck. They only have kids when they get bored fucking. Generations have nothing to say to one another. Love is just a Hollywood lie. They're all numb out there, numb or dead. But music can change the colour of the wallpaper in a room. It can raise you from your torpor, even for a moment it can make you give a shit. It's got to matter. Even if everything else in your life is a vast ocean of turd believe in what you're doing. Live and do it more. Music got to you. Live and get to other people. Fight. Fight the good fight. Tear it down – whatever 'it' is. Fight the jocks and the cheerleaders and the vacuous and the dull; show them there's more than the drab, grey limits to their tedious imaginations: please.

ONE MAN, TWO GUVNORS
by Richard Bean

This play was first performed at the National Theatre, London, on 17 May 2011.

One Man, Two Guvnors is an updated version of Carlo Goldoni's eighteenth-century Italian comedy, *Servant of Two Masters*. Set in 1960s Brighton, the Commedia character Truffaldino (the 'Servant') has been transformed into FRANCIS (the 'One Man' of the title). He is described as 'overweight' and wearing a suit that is 'too tight, too short'; he is obsessed with finding food/sating his enormous appetite. FRANCIS has just become minder to the small-time East End criminal, Roscoe Crabbe (the first 'Guvnor') and enters the stage from 'The Cricketers Arms'. On the outdoor pub tables are some unfinished drinks: Guinness, white wine, red wine in a bottle and some orange juice. FRANCIS addresses the audience directly.

FRANCIS

My father, Tommy Henshall, God rest his soul, he woulda been proud of me, what I done with my life, until today. I used to play washboard in a skiffle band, but they went to see The Beatles last Tuesday night, and sacked me Wednesday morning. Ironic, because I started the Beatles. I saw them in Hamburg. Rubbish. I said to that John Lennon, I said 'John, you're going nowhere mate, it's embarrassing, have you ever considered writing your own songs'. So I'm skint, I'm busking, guitar, mouth organ on a rack, bass drum tied to me foot, and the definition of mental illness, cymbals between my knees. So there I am, middle of Victoria Station, I've only been playing ten minutes, this lairy bloke comes over, he says – 'do you do requests?' I say 'yes' he says 'I'd like you to play a song for my mother'. I said 'no problem, where is she?' He said 'Tasmania.' So I nutted him. This little bloke Roscoe Crabbe seen all this and offers me a week's work in Brighton, says he needs a bit of muscle. I tell him this is all fat. But I need a wage. I haven't eaten since last night. And what is my first job in the criminal underworld? Walk into Charlie the Duck's house in Brighton and put the fear of God into him. Kaw! That was a bit of test for my arsehole. But it's all acting. *'Watcha! Wooa! Wot you looking at? You want some? Come on then! Eh, eh, eh, eh.'* I can do that, I'm a geezer. But I don't get paid until the end of the week, and I can't stop thinking about CHIPS. I'm staying in a pub, and I don't even have enough shrapnel for a PINT.

(He empties all the dregs into one pint pot, picks a tab end out and downs it in one. He looks at the dustbin. Puts a hand on the lid.)

There might be a discarded bag of chips in here. No! I can't go through the bins! Must stop thinking about CHIPS. Come on Francis! Think about something boring, like...CANADA.

UNTITLED
by Inua Ellams

Untitled *was produced by Fuel and Soho Theatre. The first performance took place at The Bristol Old Vic Theatre on 23 September 2010.*

Identical twin babies, born in Nigeria, are separated at seven months old. The mother takes one child (Y) and flees to England, the other (X) stays in the village with his father. However, X's life is a troubled one because his father was unable to name him, thereby denying him his destiny. Twenty-five years later, X explains (directly to the audience).

X

To name something is to call it into life and determine its future, for instance, a child named 'Freedom' is destined to roam the world, so tremendous care is taken when naming. Now, when a child is born, the father and mother never speak the name of the son or daughter, choose only on paper. When it is settled and a name takes form, the child is carried into a clearing in the forest on the night of the first full moon, lifted to light and whispered its name, that it may first know its destiny and claim it before the world does.

I was born on Independence Day. 1st of October. As Nigeria danced and villages pulsed with talking drums, I kicked into the world, but there were two of us. Identical twins. When my father who laboured far heard the news, he ran like a wind to the hut back home, for the moon was two days away and he had to name two sons. At night, he carried us gently, his bare feet crushed the forest's green, my mother – one step behind him, the path unwinding like a lock of hair to the clearing where the moon swooned down and licked the lounging leaves, passed me to my mother, lifted my brother and whispered his name. He smiled, giggled a laugh that tickled the moon who grew brighter for my turn, father lifted me to light, made to say my name, when a shadow crossed the moon for a fragment of an instance and fled. The forest's heart skipped a beat that spread into the undergrowth, rippled all trees. Father shivered, waited for the moment to pass, then lifted me to light, whispering my name…

WHAAAAAAAAAAAAAAAAA! I cried! I screamed! So
loudly, the stream ran back to the river, the moon dimmed,
the bushes curled back their ears, animals fled the forest, the
village thought The End had come. WHAAAAAAAAAA!
That night I woke up the world! It had never passed in the
village that a child rejected its destiny, its name. Father tried
six more times to name me, each time I screamed till the
Spirits cringed, seven months, seven moons in total. After that
he gave up // Let him name himself for all I care! // Mother
was unhappy // The Spirits will not stand for it, there will
be consequences // she warned…they argued, they fought.
Bitterly. He struck her. She carried my brother and left the
village. The elders said that as our parents pulled us apart, we
cried my brother and I. Our screams splintered young trees,
split two kola nuts and froze the blood as they watched. We
were just seven months old. The elders were so ashamed
they kept it a secret. That was twenty-five years ago, haven't
seen them since. So, I grew up a child with no destiny, the
unnamed one. That is how life began.

OUR CLASS

by Tadeusz Slobodzianek,
in a new version by Ryan Craig

This version of Our Class *was first performed on 16 September 2009 in the Cottesloe Theatre of the National Theatre, London.*

Poland, 1925 and we meet a class of children ambitious for the future. However, their world is split apart by invasion: first the Soviets then the Nazis. As violence escalates, the former classmates are pitted against each other. RYSIEK, planning resistance against the Soviets, believes he has been betrayed by Jakub Katz, however it was actually another classmate, Zygmunt. Later, after RYSIEK has been released, he and two of his class mates batter Jakub Katz to death on the street. Here RYSIEK describes for the audience the torture he faced at the hands of the Soviets.

RYSIEK

They took me to a room. What's your name? I said my name's
blah de blah…they said you're lying. Your name is 'Cedar'
and you are the leader of an illegal terrorist organisation called
The White Eagle. I said I didn't know what they were talking
about. They grabbed me and threw me to the floor. They
snatched my cap off my head and stuffed it in my mouth.
One man sat on my legs, while another grabbed my head. I
saw a third man reach behind a stove and pull out this cudgel.
I bit down on my cap, ready for it. He beat me, and beat me,
and beat me…I chewed my cap to shreds. Then they sat me
on this stool by a wall. They got a good grip of my hair and
smashed my head against the wall…over and over…so hard
I thought my skull would shatter. After that they yanked
out great clumps of hair. All the time they were repeating…
Confess. Give us the names of your accomplices. I knew if I
talked, the others'd get the same treatment. Better to take the
punishment on my own. I didn't know a man could take so
much.

…

Months went by. One night…must have been March or April
by now because the ground was starting to thaw…three men
came for me. They put me on a cart and drove me into the
forest. When we stopped they put a shovel in my hand and
ordered me to dig. I didn't say anything back, just started
digging. For a moment, just for a split second, as I dug, I
looked up at the sky. It was crowded with stars. And through
the mist I could just about make out the Plough. And there

was the Northern Star. And a wave of despair came over me. I felt a sorrow…for everything. For myself especially. That I had to die so young. And whose fault was it? My classmate Jakub Katz. When I dug the hole I told them I'd finished. Good, said the lieutenant, but we've decided not to shoot you today. Have a little think about things. Then confess. And when you confess you can go home. And if you don't confess, we'll bring you back here. Your pit awaits.

SHALOM BABY
by Rikki Beadle-Blair

This play was first performed at Theatre Royal Stratford East on 20 October 2011.

Shalom Baby intertwines the stories of two mixed-race couples: one from 1930s Berlin and the other from modern-day Brooklyn. Born of an African mother and German father, IKE is not 'acceptable' under Nazi rule. He becomes a shabbes goy for the Jewish Weissmann family (assisting them on the Sabbath with tasks that are forbidden to them by Jewish law) and eventually falls in love with their daughter, Natalie. Here, he explains to Herschel and Morrie Weissmann where his loyalty lies and how it was rejected by the Nazis. Later, when the Weissmanns are to be deported to a concentration camp, IKE arranges to be taken with them so he can stay with Natalie. When Natalie dies of starvation in Auschwitz, IKE hangs himself.

IKE

My father, like Aimon's – like so many – fought for this country. Gave an arm and an eye without complaint, not a bitter word. When he brought my mother to join him here, there were slammed doors, fearful silences, street abuse – but also kindness – unexpected and unsolicited. He encouraged me to claim my legacy of German strength and pride. Both the African lion and the German eagle, he'd say. Roar and Soar. When I first heard Hitler speak, like so many other German children I was electrified, inspired. At last a voice in the wilderness that called for a return to strength and pride. Roar and soar. I wanted a Hitler Youth uniform more than almost anything. They made everyone who wore them seem so much taller, as solid and certain as trees. They had finally arrived – the next evolution. The Supermen. When I attempted to enlist and was told that I was racially unsuitable – genetically flawed – I was devastated and utterly confused. I knew no other language. I had never even left the country. Yet they were saying that my blood that I was so willing to spill for the Fatherland, was of no value. When my father found me weeping, he told me, 'Where you belong is for no other man to decide… This is your world, claim the country that calls you – it's between you and the Earth'.

BEA

by Mick Gordon

This play was first performed at Soho Theatre in London on 1 December 2010.

Bea, in her late twenties, has a chronically debilitating illness and needs constant care. Bea's mother, Katherine, is a barrister and cannot look after her so she employs RAY as Bea's carer. RAY is in his mid-twenties and, back home in Northern Ireland, has a sister, Sandra, who is autistic. When Bea decides she no longer wants to live, it is RAY who, ultimately, helps Katherine understand. This speech explores his horror of confinement, clearly empathising with Bea's physical confinement. RAY's departure soon after helps Katherine to take the next step and set Bea free.

RAY

I was in prison once. Well, borstal. It was because I...well,
I suppose it was attention seeking really, what with Sandra,
and I just felt, well sort of ignored I suppose. I know it wasn't
their fault, it's no fun what they went through, they lost
their lives to Sandra and I, well I was young then wasn't I
and I didn't understand and...well you know, one thing led
to another and then to another and then before I knew it I
was standing in an Elton John mask robbing the Nationwide.
Not on my own like. I had friends. Bruce Springstein, who
was actually called Bruce, we had a big argument about
that but he wouldn't be told, Frank Sinatra, who was called
Jeremy – Jezzer, Rodge was Tina Turner, always been fiercely
independent Mr. Dodge – and done very well – I was telling
Bea, and Freddy Krueger who was an extremely short boy
called Bonehead. We were inspired by that movie where they
dress up as the ex-presidents, you know – the surfers and
sky-divers and stuff but we just used mum's Mini Metro,
anyway, we got caught. Bonehead cut his hand on his penknife, Bruce had painted his water-pistol black but he hadn't
let it dry properly and his hand got stuck to it. He looked,
well frankly, he looked ridiculous. Jezzer, well, Jez couldn't
see out of his mask properly because he's got a very small face
and Frank Sinatra's face is surprisingly big so he couldn't see
where he was going and ended up trying to rob the Kentucky
Fried Chicken next door. And I actually had a panic attack
so couldn't get the car keys out of my pocket. Rodge was the
only one who escaped, because he was so good at running.
He's still got Tina somewhere. But the rest of us, caught red-

handed, except for Bruce obviously. It was a dark day. We all got time. But Borstal, let me tell you, that was the real low point for me. On my second night the boy in the next cell hung himself, hanged? Hung. Yeah, he'd ripped up the bed-sheet, and that's very hard to do because they're not normal sheets, they're reinforced with something, so that must have meant he really wanted to do it. It's the locks. And the doors. But mostly the locks. That's all you hear, clunking you in. K-lunk. K-lunk. And they echo. The sound gets further away each time and you quietly realise how totally trapped you are. When you understand what the word confined actually means. Confined. It's the worst feeling I've ever, no, no not the worst, the second worst. The worst was, the worst was the night when I suddenly knew, exactly, how that boy next door had been feeling. I'm sitting on my bed looking down at my shoes. And I caught myself wishing there were laces in them. That was it. The most shocking moment of my entire life. I think it was the shock that saved me. It could have gone either way but for some reason I decided then and there I would survive. Don't know why but from then on best behaviour. Best behaviour. And that's probably why I'm a nurse, care assistant, even more than Sandra. Just hard to put it on a CV, you know. I mean you can't – took some fiddling that Mrs. James, I can tell you – and good news – I've got another job. And I'm going to take it so I probably won't be seeing either of you again.

LOWER NINTH
by Beau Willimon

Lower Ninth *was originally presented at The Acorn Theatre as
part of the Summer Play Festival in New York City, opening on
10 July 2007. The world premiere was at The Flea Theater in
New York City on 28 February 2008. The UK premiere was at
the Donmar Warehouse, London, on 30 September 2010.*

New Orleans has been devastated by floods and two African
Americans, Malcom (mid-forties) and E-Z (mid-twenties), are
stranded on a rooftop, surrounded by water, awaiting rescue.
Their only companion is the dead body of their friend, Lowboy,
who didn't make it when the waters rose. In this scene, E-Z
tells Malcom about a very different time when he was stranded.

E-Z

Reminds me of this time, this field trip we went on when I
was a kid. Out to the swamp. We all on those boats – you
know? Those ones with the big fans? Fly on top of the water?

…

Right. So we all on these boats and we stop on this little island
for lunch. Some park ranger man is tellin' us 'bout nature,
'bout the crocs and whatnot, the birds, all the animals all
'round. But I gotta take myself a crap. I mean *real* bad. So I
go on over into some trees a ways off, so nobody don't see me,
and I take my crap, wipe my ass with a leaf and shit. Problem
is, when I come back all the kids, the boats, they gone. There
I am on this little island ain't no one around. So I figure I just
wait, you know? Can't be long 'fore they figure I'm missin'.
But shit man, an hour goes by, then another, and another. Sun
starts goin' down. I'm scared to death, little kid like me all
alone in the swamp there. But after a while I come to like the
place. Like I got my very own island all to myself. Like I'm the
king of this island, and can't no one tell me what to do. Figure
I can get some branches together, make myself a nice little
hut. Make some fishing line outta the vines and shit. Weave
myself some baskets outta the marsh grass to collect me some
rainwater. Live there till I'm an old man. Dig my own grave
and lie down in it my day come to die. I start hopin' they
don't never find me. Just leave me right where I am. Like I'm
a king, you know? King of this island an it ain't nobody's but
mine.

E-Z chuckles. A pause.

...

Yeah man, they find me. Not that I helped 'em none. Night time come along and I hear the big ole fan boats comin', see the search lights, hear folks callin' my name. So what I do is hide myself in some bushes and hope they pass me on by. But those boats come right up to the island and all these park rangers come stomping through with flashlights. Wasn't long 'fore they had me back in one of those boats. And man, did momma give me a whoopin'.

...

Teacher blamed it on me though. Said I shouldn't have wandered off. And who you think my Mama's gonna listen to? So I tell her 'What? I was just s'posed to crap myself?' And that pissed her off even more. So yeah, I got myself a whoopin' good.

...

This roof here ain't no place for a king.

LOVE STEALS US FROM LONELINESS

by Gary Owen

This play was commissioned and produced by the National Theatre Wales and its first performance was at Hobos, Bridgend on 7 October 2010.

Set in Bridgend in Wales, *Love Steals Us from Loneliness* focuses on the family and friends of a teenager (Lee) killed in a car accident. SCOTT was Lee's best friend. He confessed love for Catrin, Lee's girlfriend, and kissed her. Catrin told Lee and, consequently, Lee stormed off in his car. This excerpt occurs in the second half of the play when SCOTT remembers back to a time when he, Welly, Huw, Rob and Lee made a pact that whoever died first would send a message to the others (proving there was life after death). However, after Lee's death, the message didn't come at the agreed time.

SCOTT

We used to go for chips every dinner time.
We'd cross Merthyr Mawr Road, then cut in the back of the
tennis club.
Then by the side of the river, into town.
There was a chip shop with a pool hall above.
It's a rock club now.
You may know it.
We'd bomb down there and wander back
Stopping on the bridge, sitting on the stones in Newbridge
Fields for a bit
With chip cones steaming off vinegar in our hands.
One day you said
D'you think you go on after you die?
Or is that just it, once you're gone you're gone?
You said, it'd be handy to know either way.
But so far no-one in history had figured it out.
And you said
Well then boys.
Looks like it's down to us.
We decided that whoever ghosted first should return and
Using our poltergeist powers turn off a light
On October the tenth, at ten o'clock precisely.
The tenth of the tenth at ten.
All the tens, you said.
Never gonna forget that, are we?
We spat in our hands and shook: I shook Welly's hand,
Welly shook Rob's hand, Rob shook Huw McArthur's, Huw
McArthur shook yours, and then you shook mine

And shaking spit round the gang
Sealed our oath –
That for the rest of our lives, on the tenth of the tenth, at ten
We would all be looking out
For a message from the dead, in the dying of an electric light.
And then we all had to finish our chips eating with the wrong hands
Cos our right hands were covered in spit.

…

And yeah
That first year
On the tenth of the tenth, at ten
I was on the look-out.

THE DARK THINGS
by Ursula Rani Sarma

*This play was first performed at the Traverse Theatre,
Edinburgh on 6 October 2009.*

DANIEL is an artist in his twenties. He has survived a horrific
bus crash and is tormented by the fact that he was the only
person who walked away. There was one other survivor, LJ,
who lost both her legs. This monologue occurs at the start of
the play and DANIEL is filming himself in a wasteland littered
with bus fragments. It is his attempt to come to terms with the
experience. He likens the crash to a moment in his childhood
when he was drowning in a lake and his sister's voice helped
him to the surface.

DANIEL

Darkness. *(Beat.)* Total and complete darkness. *(Beat.)*
Oceanic darkness *(Beat.)* Like being at the bottom of a lake,
on your back, stuck fast in the mud and sinking *(Beat.)* Trying
to breathe, trying to decide if I am alive or dead, try telling
myself it's a dream and will myself to wake up and see…
and see…my bedside table…yellow lamp…floral sheets
(Beat.) comforting. *(Beat.)* No. *(Beat.)* Then tell myself I'm
drowning because I know that feeling…drowning…this…
being…crushed, lungs being crushed, collapsing, no air, stuck
fast in the mud and…drowning. *(Beat.)* Before…there was a
woman beside me, bright coloured clothes, baby strapped to
her chest, smiling, happy, made me smile without meaning
to. *(Beat.)* There was a girl by the door with long red hair and
her face was covered in freckles…and her skin…looked like
porcelain…pale…translucent. She was very thin…looked like
she could break easily…delicate…made me want to protect
her. *(Beat.)* In that heat…everything seemed that little bit
more…intense and colourful and I smiled at this red haired
girl and she smiled back and the city didn't feel like a city,
it felt like we all wanted the same things in the end…and
it was a good feeling…warm and comforting and good and
then *(Beat.)* Darkness. *(Beat.)* Metal scraping and collapsing
and the bus seats buckling and people screaming. *(Beat.)*
My eyes closing and not re-opening *(Beat.)* Heaving…things
snapping…breaking…things being broken…bones…no…yes
bones. *(Beat.)* The sound of bones breaking is…inhuman. I
curl up…in a ball…pull my knees up duck my head down and
pray…please God get me out of this…please God…please

fucking God… I don't care… I don't care if everyone else is crushed to death and I'm… I'm the only one left.

…

And then I hear a voice…calling me and it's a familiar voice… it sounds comforting…and it's coming from above…and more than anything…I want to be near that voice. *(Beat.)* And I will myself to move…will my lungs to inflate and push outwards and push upwards…force my bones up towards the voice… towards the light beyond the darkness and beyond the metal scraping bone breaking…and then the voice gets louder and louder until it kind of… *(Relishing the moment.)* wraps itself around me…and it is heat and comfort and safety and home…

BEARDY
by Tom Wells

Taken from *SIXTY-SIX BOOKS: 21ˢᵗ-Century Writers Speak to the King James Bible*

Sixty-Six Books: 21ˢᵗ-Century Writers Speak to the King James Bible *was first performed at the Bush Theatre in London on 10 October 2011. On 14 and 28 October, the sixty-six texts were performed back-to-back in an all-night vigil at the Bush. On 28 October they were performed complete at Westminster Abbey.*

Sixty-Six Books is a celebration of the 400ᵗʰ anniversary of the King James Version of the Bible. Sixty-six writers were commissioned to interpret a book from the KJV for the twenty-first century. They include playwrights, poets, novelists and songwriters differing in gender, age, ethnicity, sexual orientation and faith. Tom Wells has turned Sansom in the Book of Judges into SAM, the strong man in a circus, who loves the bearded lady, Debbie. The lion is dead, killed by SAM, and he has been told to dress up as a replacement lion. However, after losing Debbie, SAM is prepared to bring the circus down, crashing onto everybody.

SAM

Sheila Beef's answer to not having a lion is to dress me up as a lion. Lock me in the cage. Hide me round the back of the Big Tent.

'Ready for the finale,' she says. Rubbing her hands.

I'm not that into it as a plan.

Try telling her I'm here to be big and, and strong. Got to put my little shorts on, do some heavy lifting but she just, dunno. Picks her whip up. Disappears.

I can hear the crowd going in. They're well rowdy. Cos it's the last night and everything. Debbie's getting the worst of it. She's in the ticket booth, there's all these pissed-up lads asking to tug her face. Hear them shouting: 'give us a kiss then,' wolf whistling and that. Women won't go near her in case they catch a beard. Kids just look at her, burst into tears.

And the Big Tent's filling up, creaking and groaning, sagging, on its last legs sort of thing but Sheila Beef's not fussed cos: showtime. She's got the Spangles warming up, chucking the Little One backwards and forwards, spinning him, bouncing him and that. Trapezey Pete's having a wee. There's a little gap in the line where Sad Jimmy would've stood. Sheila Beef's inside, whipping the crowd up. Cheering, clapping, stamping. It's a bit much, to be honest, all this noise. Start to panic a bit. Cos I don't mind doing the strong man stuff but this is all, this is a bit new. And Debbie must know I'm worried cos she comes to see me.

'You alright?'

Make a face like 'not really' but she's a bit distracted to be honest. I think it's one of those times when she's not really wanting to know if I'm alright or not. Sometimes it's just something you say. And Debbie's all edgy and that, looking over her shoulder, breathing fast.

'I need you to do me a favour', she says.

And I'm like: 'course.'

'Need you to buy me some time.'

She's got all the ticket money with her, and Sad Jimmy's razor so I can, I sort of work it out, what's going on. And it's. Um. I dunno.

'Will you do that for me Sam?

So, yeah. I just:

Slow, sad nod.

And she leans in through the bars, Debbie, and she kisses me. Just a tiny kiss, like a blink really, a flutter. Feel her lovely soft beard on the side of my face, much softer than I expected.

And she's gone.

Cos she wants to be ordinary, Debbie. More than anything.

I reckon she couldn't be ordinary if she tried. Reckon she's too wonderful but.

But it doesn't really matter what I think.

*

I'm not that good at being a lion.

Especially since they were all expecting a real lion. I'm just a tit in a furry top.

Try to roar a bit but. Won't come out.

The crowd are getting angry now, hammering with their feet, chucking all these empty cans, full cans, rocks and that, anything they've got. They think that's alright, an alright thing to do. Think it's fair enough. And Sheila Beef's still here, whipping. Getting them all wound up. Tent's groaning like a shipwreck, splinters dropping from the ceiling. It's about done in. Just want it to stop really.

So what I do: I think about Debbie.

Think about how her life'll be better and that. Without this. No beard and, and with her bungalow and her BTEC and everything. Hope she'll manage it. Cos it's hard work really, holding a life together. If no one's shown you how. Difficult, I think.

And I think there's, there's a way I can help her, hopefully.

So I'm eyeing up the pole in the middle of the Big Tent, holds it all up. Thinking: probably as rotten as the rest. One good shove I reckon. Whole lot'll be crashing down. This lot inside and, and me in the middle.

And I don't want to do it really. But. I dunno it's. It's the best I've got.

Try to feel peaceful. Strong.

And I push, and I push, and I push.

PART THREE:
THIRTIES

MIDDLETOWN
by Will Eno

Middletown was first performed at the Vineyard Theatre in New York City on 3 November 2010 and won the Horton Foote Prize 2011.

This play focuses on how humanity ekes out an existence in small-town America. The MECHANIC is in his late twenties/ early thirties and drinks to lessen the emotional pain of living. He can often be found on a bench, drinking a bottle out of a paper bag. In this monologue he tries to explain himself to the audience.

MECHANIC

…I'm nothing special, post-natally speaking. I fix cars, I try to.
I get hassled by the cops, try to maintain a certain – I don't
know – sobriety. Sometimes, I volunteer at the hospital, dress
up for the kids. It was part of a plea deal. But what isn't.
Nothing really crazy to report. Except, I found this rock once,
everyone. What I thought was a meteorite. I brought the
thing into the school, here. The kids ran it through all these
tests, tapped on it, shined lights at it. I found it in a field. It
looked special. Then the astronaut here told me it was just a
rock. Said it was probably from, at some earlier time, another
slightly larger rock. His name is Greg Something. I had ideas
about getting famous, getting on local TV with my meteorite.
When it turned out to just be a rock, I thought I could still
make some headlines with it if I threw it off a bridge, hit
some family in their car and killed everybody. But then I
figured, you know what, forget it, that's not me. So now some
family's driving around, not knowing how lucky they are, not
knowing how sweet it all is. Just because. *(Very brief pause.)*
Wait, hang on a second. Do you… *(Pause. He stays very still
and listens intently.)* I thought I heard something. *(Listens
again for a moment.)* I'm still not convinced I didn't. Weird.
Anyway, that was just a little local story. Although, you know,
it almost had outer space in it. *(Brief pause.)* I wish that lady
luck, with the family. People don't stop to think of how lucky
they are. I do. And, I've realized, I'm not that lucky. But I get
by. If I had more self-esteem, more stick-to-itiveness, I might
have been a murderer. I was a child once. Like everybody.
Some worried mother's son or distant father's daughter,

sneaking around with a dirty face and an idea. My hand was this big. *(With thumb and forefinger he indicates the size of an infant's hand. About an inch and a half.)* I was somebody's golden child, somebody's little hope. Now, I'm more just, you know, a local resident. Another earthling.

IN THE PIPELINE
by Gary Owen

In the Pipeline *was first presented by Radio Wales in April 2005.*

A large gas pipeline is going to be laid through the Pembrokeshire countryside in Wales. *In the Pipeline* allows three characters who will be caught in its path to have their say. ANDREW works on the railways, pushing the tea trolley up and down the train. He hasn't lived in his village very long and, despite visiting the pubs on a regular basis, hasn't bonded with anyone there. He isn't particularly worried about the pipeline and has plans to sell up to the gas company, that is, before he meets Alison.

ANDREW

When Alison moved in over the road I thought I had a chance.

Not a chance with her. But a chance to be a bit different, now I wasn't the newest person in the village.

First I thought I'd go over, introduce myself as she was unpacking, maybe lend a hand with the boxes and crates. But I'm not the world's most dextrous person. I drop things.

Plus she had a kid. A little girl, about five or six.

A grown-up will say at worst, that you're looking nice and healthy. A kid will just go – why's that man so fat, mummy?

So I thought best not.

Then one night I come into the Red Lion, having had the full quota of two in the Bull and two in the King's Head, and Alison's there. Sitting on her own. No kid, no boyfriend, no nothing.

And without thinking about it I make myself go up to her. And I say, hiya.

She looks at me a bit funny and I say, sorry – I live opposite you. And she's all yes of course you do, and I go, no, no reason why you should recognise me, I just thought I'd say hello.

Welcome you to the village.

Great, she says. Are you – on your own?

Am as it happens, I say.

Well d'you wanna join me, she goes.

I say, yeah, that'd be nice –

– and as I'm saying it, she goes, you can introduce me to some of the locals maybe?

And of course I can't do that. Cause I don't know any of them.

So I sort of slap on my thigh. And pull out my phone. And stare at it a bit.

I say, sorry, bit of an emergency at work. I'm gonna have to go.

Right, she says. Well perhaps another time.

Yeah perhaps, I go.

Of course what this little exchange tells me is that she's the friendly type. So she's bound to get talking to people, and she'll say who was that bloke who was in here earlier, who went to sit down with me and then rushed out. And everyone in the pub will say – we don't know. He's just this bloke who comes in, half-cut, sits on his own, sinks two pints, and shuffles off home.

I gave up on Alison then. She would smile at me, across the road, but – it was, you know.

DEEP HEAT
by Robin Soans

Selections from Deep Heat *were first performed at a National Theatre Platform in London on 9 May 2011.*

Deep Heat, *subtitled* 'Encounters with the Famous, the Infamous and the Unknown', contains verbatim monologues collected and edited by Robin Soans. The following excerpt is the written voice of PAUL, a thirty-year-old heroin addict from Leeds. Here, he tells the story of how his best (and only) friend died.

PAUL

Rattling or off your head...that's when you get caught. I
went into the Co-op, pulled a gun, off my nut on crack. I
took a few hundred quid, but I left too big a slit. The girl
on the till recognised me. She got the eyes. That's how I
got done. I got eight years for that. I'd been out ten weeks,
and I got done for two shopliftings and a burglary...so I was
back inside for fifteen months...out in February last year...
back in a flat for a while, but I've got an electronic tag on my
ankle, so if I go out after the curfew, the alarm goes off in the
police station. And I'm back on the gear. By this time I've
used up all my veins, and I've got these track marks in my
neck. You have to get someone else to dig you in the neck...
you can't do it yourself...you might end up puncturing your
windpipe. Me and my mate Andy used to dig each other in
the neck. He's hobbling by this time, using a stick, 'cos one
day, when I was still inside, he'd injected crushed up sleeping
pills into his groin. You need a number two needle...it's like
a chalky solution, it won't go through a number one needle...
and you literally have to whack it in you. He's got it in, and
it's clogged his veins up...the smaller veins in his foot...and
he's got gangrene. They've taken four toes off one foot. So
this one time he phones me...he's rattling, got no money...
he says, 'Have you got any stuff?' I've just had a dig...in mi
arse, which is about the only place I've not been...and all I've
got left is the wash...the residue left in the spoon...the shit
basically. He says, 'That'll do, I'm coming round.' He hobbles
in, puts his stick down; I sucked up the wash into the syringe,
and I dig him in the neck. He starts going doolally, shouting all

sorts and hops out…out of his mind. I can't follow cos I've got this electronic tag on mi leg. Twenty minutes later his mum phones. She's panicking saying he's gone completely doolally, like he needs help urgently, I thought, 'Fuck it' and run out of the house. I found him outside the block of flats where he lived. He's thrown himself on to a metal fence. The spikes have gone through his chest. There's blood coming from his nose and ears. I have to physically lift him off. He's dead. This is my one and only best mate, and I've killed him. I told the police the first I knew was when his mum phoned for help.

CHEKHOV IN HELL
by Dan Rebellato

Chekhov in Hell *was first performed at the Drum Theatre Plymouth on 4 November 2010.*

This play follows the experiences of the Russian playwright Anton Chekhov after he wakes up from a coma in an NHS hospital in the 21st Century. Chekhov was a keen observer of late nineteenth-century life and he employs the same detailed fascination with some of the more ridiculous, superficial and incongruous elements within contemporary society. This includes the fashion world in a scene entitled 'Yo Soy un Fashionista'. MAX is in his mid-30s and works for an important fashion house. He thinks Chekhov is a journalist and therefore presents him with some of the company designs on a showroom model. Although this scene excerpt includes responses/questions from Chekhov, it can easily be turned into a monologue.

MAX

This showroom cost a fortune to do up. Brushed steel and curved red stained-glass which some people say 'what are we, Japafuckinese?' and I say, 'Tokyo is the future, honey, get used to it.'

The model comes in again.

Okay so. In three years, we're going to be very bored of real and we're going to remember – at *last*, let me say – that artificial is the funnest thing.

We're going to be seeing a *lot* of fun fur edging. Bags, tops, coats, shoes. And we're going to bring back, yes, colour! Neons again, puffball skirts – which so obvious but hey obvious starts getting sexy next Spring – we're thinking satsuma, lime green, Tizer colours. And for that extra flash, we're going right back to tube socks but that is super-ultra secret and if you tell anyone I will *personally* burn your house down.

[ANTON: You know all this now.]

MAX: Sure. You have to order the dyes at least three years in advance, so we have to choose the colours way before that.

[ANTON: You are like a wizard. You know what ladies want to wear in the future.]

MAX: Let me tell you a secret.

[ANTON: Please.]

MAX: Women are
That's OK Mimi.
(Confidentially.) Women are stupid.

[ANTON: They are?]

MAX: Uh huh. Like real deep down stupid.
Now sure I wouldn't say this if there were any of them here,
but between us.
But okay every year we come up with some new type of thing
for them to wear. And every year it's something really stupid-
looking, ugly, uncomfortable, whatever. Something just kind
of ridiculous maybe. And what do they do?
They buy it. They wear it. But it gets better: they want to buy
it, they want to wear it.

[ANTON: They do?]

MAX: Women are giving it all about equality bla bla and
they're getting the top jobs and big salaries, deep down they
are stupid and we know that and fashion is our way, as men, to
remind each other of this fact.

[ANTON: You believe this?]

MAX: Let me give you an example. Ten years ago we decided
– it was a kind of joke actually, over a bottle of wine in Milan
– to revolutionise underwear. Knickers out, thongs in. All
women must wear thongs – no other underwear is acceptable.
And this guy, he's from Moncelli's in Florence, he says to us:
and why don't we bring back hipsters at the same time? Low
cut, deep waist, hipster jeans.
And we were like no fucking *way*, that is *totally* a step too
far. Because you can't have the hipster cut and the thong, it's
either one or the other.

But it worked. Women bought both.

And you know what else?

It became sexy.

You see a girl in low-cut jeans and a thong, you get a semi going on, you know what I mean?

And why?

Because the fact that women are so easy to dominate is the biggest fucking turn on ever.

I love your look, girlfriend. Vintage works now.

You want a bit of crank? Bit of Tina? I can go for hours.

Help yourself to the biscuits, they're from Iceland. They're a statement.

WE'RE GONNA MAKE YOU WHOLE
by Yasmine Van Wilt

We're Gonna Make You Whole *was first performed at the Acquire Arts in Battersea, London on 10 August 2011.*

This play is based on the true-life testimonies of Louisiana residents who were affected by a major petrochemical disaster. CURTIS LAFONTAINE is in his late twenties/early thirties. He worked on the oil rig when it exploded and has been affected physically and emotionally. He is, however, unable to claim significant compensation because he signed a waiver presented to him immediately after the accident when he was still in a state of shock. In this scene, he is being interviewed about his experiences for a local news programme.

CURTIS

Well...I woke up to an explosion. I turned and I sat at the edge of ma bed. I'm... And the force – clear threw me across my room – into the fire-rated doors. These are three-inch thick, steel-doors...and it clear knocked me out. When I came to, smoke was already eating into the room and...I was bleeding from...what I know now was my head. And it was...thick, like pudding – just coming down into my eyes. I finally managed to get out onto the deck of the rig. Where I got slammed again by flying debris – clear knocked me to the floor below. And at this point, there are petroleum cans, and greasers, and all sorts of things which we use...every day to keep our systems ticking. And they were all exploding, like the most intense fire-crackers you could imagine. It was like... it was like...Baghdad on the deck... When I finally managed to make my way down to the derrick – to the fire station – it was consumed by fire, it was like... I knew there was no way we were gonna put that out. I knew we should abandon the rig...

...

I was still kinda in shock. The main thing going through my head was – we're all dead. There's no way we're getting' off here. As we were getting our gear on...we saw the crane operator get knocked forty, fifty feet from the derrick, clean to the bottom of the deck. *(Beat.)* We dressed out as fast as – We started trying to make our way over to get him...and flames surrounded us in every direction...and there was no way we could get him. *(A pause.)* We...I...had to leave him.

...

(He gulps. He clears his throat. He is nearly sweating he is so distressed…) It was…the worst…thing I've ever had to do. It haunts me today… I can't stop asking myself…is there any other way I coulda gotten over there?

A pause.

…

I mean…you know, it burns a hole inside you, losing one of your own…But, we know it's…part of what we're trained to expect…part of – what we know could happen. Losing someone we're meant to protect. Somehow it's worse. And it ain't like – they was just members of the public. Losing someone is never easy…it always feels like you've failed – But on a rig – you're a family. Eighteen hours a day, every day… you ain't got your wife and kids around, you got – your… *(He falters, for lack of a better word.)*…people become –

…

Well…when it came down to the day. The actual fire. Nothing went like it was supposed to. There were…problems in the engine room. The blowout preventer… That's supposed to – well stop a blowout – and to isolate the rig – and that didn't work, obviously. And then, also, none of the fire-safety mechanisms worked either. So, basically, all the things which were meant to keep us safe, turned on us… It was just us men – fighting that fire, with basic equipment.

ZERO
by Chris O'Connell

Zero was produced by Theatre Absolute in conjunction with Warwick Arts Centre in Coventry, where it was first performed on 29 September 2008.

This play is set twenty years into a brutal future, where hundreds of detainee camps have been set up around the world to obtain information at any cost from terrorists and suspected terrorists. DEMISSIE is an inmate in one of these camps, subjected to constant torture. Alex is a translator there and finds conditions confronting and intolerable. In this scene, DEMISSIE finally starts talking. He tells Alex exactly why he did what he did.

DEMISSIE

Lately, I feel, I am more and more vile. Poisoned, perhaps. But not always. In a different life I have been, or was…pleasant, hard working. I owned a garage, I fixed the vehicles of all the diplomats in the city. Fifteen years of my life, and plans for more garages. Plans to become a 'Business Man'. Three years ago, the Embassy announced that its work would be put out to tender, and they gave the contract to a foreign company. My tender was cheaper, but this company's business was well known, they have their headquarters in the city, they own oil, and water, and other utilities over a huge region of the country.

[ALEX: Economics, / it's…]

DEMISSIE: Yes. And I'm laughed at when I try to tell people that I can fix the cars as well as this company. Since when did they care about cars? I am a native of the city, and this company is foreign, coming and going as it pleases. But its garages are plush, they're new. I approach people in the street who look important, and I try to persuade them to bring their cars to me. They ask for a card. I say I don't have one. They ask for my website address, I say I don't have one. But I understand that I need one, that to compete with this company I should buy my clothes from Paris, or my shoes from London, and I don't have the money. All my life, money invades my dreams, hallucinates me, it takes away my reason because I know I will gladly kiss the feet of The Rich if it means I too can be like them. And now, just to survive, I realise I need more money than I ever could imagine. What has happened to Demissie? My wife is offered work at the Embassy; she works in the kitchens, what little she earns keeps us afloat, and I continue with my efforts to bring business back to my garage. I decide to buy new equipment, but the bank won't give me money. By the end of the day, I understand that I am alone, and when you are alone, it is easier to act alone. Friends I talked to before, many had experiences like mine, they were angry, they talked of action. Listening to them, I was unsure. But now I borrow money from a back street loan agency, and I buy explosives and guns from the internet.

[ALEX: Why didn't you use it to buy the new equipment you needed?

DEMISSIE stops, he smiles.]

DEMISSIE: I'm not sure what I will do with these new toys, but I feel a satisfaction in my belly, that I have done something. At the Embassy, my wife works on an important party, and at the end of the night she is stopped at the embassy gates as she leaves with a bag of food that was left uneaten. She explains that her supervisor said to take the food home, but the Embassy's guards say she stole it.

[ALEX: Did she?]

DEMISSIE: Why would my wife steal?

[*No answer.*]

The guards laugh and they make her watch as they throw the food to their dogs. It was difficult to sleep. I was haunted by the truth of what it meant for us to have become so worthless, that the Embassy's dogs were better fed than my family. One week after, the company who won the tender had too much work, and one of the diplomats for the Embassy came back to my garage. I put a bomb under his car, and one hour later it detonated and killed him.

UP ON ROOF

by *Richard Bean*

from *Bean Plays Three*

This play was first performed at Hull Truck Theatre on 5 March 2006.

It is 1976 and there is a riot in Hull prison. A few of the prisoners have made their way to the prison roof. Thirty-year-old CHRISTOPHER also makes his way there, wearing new, still creased, prison-issue clothes. He tells the other prisoners that he only recently arrived (having been accused of murdering his father) and was just being moved to a cell when the riot broke out. Later on in the play the prisoners believe he might be a plant. In this excerpt, one of the prisoners has just asked CHRISTOPHER how he would escape so he explains his ideal plan. There is an exchange of dialogue during the scene (deleted material is indicated by '…'); however the story does work well as a monologue.

CHRISTOPHER

I'd walk straight out the door.

…

Every day a hundred, I guess maybe two hundred people walk straight in this prison, and at the end of the day, they walk straight out again.

…

Even with all those cameras, and doors, and rivers to ford, and mountains to climb, and seas to swim – every day a hundred people escape this prison.

…

Over time you –

…

You develop a relationship with the Art Teacher.

…

You fall in love with her. She falls in love with you. In the art class you kiss in the paint cupboard, quick frantic embraces – a lust made more driven and desperate because it cannot be consummated.

…

She'll do anything for you. Every now and then you achieve a surreptitious caress.

…

You study her. Her voice. Her face. Her legs. Her smell. The way she talks. The way she smiles, stands, scratches, sniffs, sighs, yawns, laughs. Alone in your cell, you practice talking like her. You teach yourself how to walk in high heels.

...

She brings in her measurements. Inside leg, hips, waist, bust. You give her yours. You make a pair of breasts.

...

The day of the escape is set, a long way off, a year ahead. She grows her hair, long, down over her eyes, covering the eye lashes, the ears.

...

When it's long she has it all cut off and has a wig made from the cut hair, and she starts to grow it long again. You grow your nails.

...

When her hair is long again, they're ready.

...

The week before the escape she has a car crash. Suffers whiplash. She has to wear one of those big collars round her neck.

...

She's also bruised about the face, or says she is –

...

So she wears very heavy make up for that week. Ostensibly to cover the bruising.

…

On the day of the escape you shave your head, your legs, the backs of your hands. She wears a two piece suit. Skirt and jacket. Shows a lot of leg. The clothes are a bit too big for her, but big enough for you. Shoes, a bit too big for her but big enough for you. Coming into the prison she wears the wig over her own long hair. She brings in make up, nail varnish; she wears distinctive dangly ear rings; carries a unique briefcase. At the end of the art class, in the paint cupboard, she undresses. You undress. *(Beat.)* You put on her clothes, and –

…

You put on the wig. She paints your nails. She does your lipstick. The heavy make up. You put on the whiplash collar. Then…

…

Then you punch her in the face. You smash her nose. With a knife you cut her arm. You draw blood. You tie her up. Unpleasantly tight. You gag her with duck tape. You punch her again. You break the skin.

…

Then you kiss her. On the lips. Lovingly.

…

You leave. You walk out the prison, the same way she walked in.

...

'You' are now 'she'.

I HEART MATHS

from

THE EGO PLAYS

by James Ley

I Heart Maths *was developed by Glasgay!, Ros Philips and acting students at the RSAMD. It was first performed on 23 May 2011 for A Play, A Pie and A Pint at Oran More, Glasgow.*

MICHAEL is a bio-mathematics lecturer at the University of Manchester and has just been cheated on by his boyfriend. Rather than dealing with his pain, he tries to come up with a mathematical formula for the ideal relationship. This is the opening monologue when he stands in front of a packed lecture theatre soon after discovering his boyfriend's affair. He has just written the following words/equations on the whiteboard – 'Derivations', 'Deleterious', 'Ploidy', 'Monoploid number', '$x = n = 23$', 'Mutation Selection Balance'.

MICHAEL

Bio-mathematicians. Third years. Fellow adults. Those who
have given up growing marijuana and now grow beards,
consult IFAs and spend your student loans on buy-to-let
mortgages. You no longer drink on a Monday night and prefer
a Soy Chai Latte and a flick through *The Independent*. I think
you're ready for a challenge. *(Beat.)* Derivations, anyone?
What's that doing up there? Where did it come from?
Deleterious – just a poncey word for harmful. Can also mean
subversive. Ploidy – possibly the best word in the English
language – just means the number of sets of chromosomes in a
biological cell. From it we get the haploid number, n, and the
monoploid number, x. Who can tell me about $x = n = 23$?
What does it express? Is it an energy drink? A new bar on the
south side? Anyone?

...

$x = n = 23$ = Man or to give us our post 19th-century title,
the human being. Now, you'll have realised by now that you
have to do an awful lot of maths before you get to the sexy
stuff but d'you know what, I think we've arrived. We're in the
mathematic bedroom. And we're finally rid of the bimbos, the
dimbos, the Oxbridge rejects, the trust fund timewasters, the
far-too-pissed-even-by-academic-standards. The am drams,
the unplanned prams, the random woman who changed to
nursery nursing, the guy with the gun, that girl, Jennifer,
who had all those accidents in the first year – god rest her
soul – and of course the dearly deported. Because although
education might seem like a good way to escape a life of

poverty and persecution, the fees can be a bit prohibitive. Anyway, it's time for me to share what is unquestionably the most important principle in the field of mathematical probability. Sadly, it can also be a little depressing. It's the reason that several of you have to do re-sits. It's why I've just taken rather a lot of time off work to recover from the shock of arriving home one evening and finding someone who wasn't supposed to be in my bedroom, in my bedroom – And I don't mean a burglar. I mean an additional person to Adam was there. I mean Adam was shagging someone else. In my bed. I mean shit happens. Or haploids, as we might say when speaking in terms of chromosomes. That's a little bio-mathematic joke for you. Because shit happens we can try to work out when, why and how shit doesn't happen. We can take the shit, and make something out of it. *(Beat.)* Does anybody have any questions? *(Beat.)* I do. I want to know why. I'm not doing all this maths for the fun of it. I'm not Carol Vorderman. Of course you'll have heard me quote, many times, The Count from *Sesame Street*, with the words 'Ha, ha, ha, I love counting!' But things have happened lately that mean I can't say that. I just can't. *(Pause.)* For this, and various other reasons, I have initiated a research project to discover why my $x = n = 23$ human being was a cheat. I want to find a way of steering clear of mutated relationships in the future. Obviously the University of Manchester won't be funding this particular study which is why, I'm afraid, I'm leaving the faculty. You will have a shiny new lecturer from Monday, who isn't falling apart at the seams. *(Beat.)* Now, I feel like I'm breaking up with you. I suppose I am. *(Grabbing his briefcase.)* I'm no good at goodbyes. Good luck.

THE MIRACLE MAN
by Douglas Maxwell

*This play was first performed at the Tron Theatre, Glasgow
in a National Theatre of Scotland production
on 10 March 2010.*

OSSIAN MACDONALD (OZZY) is a thirty-something-year-old PE teacher with a famous father who is dying of cancer. He is drawn to a group of teens in his school who are struggling to find their identity (albeit through a cult that demands a virginity pledge). However, it is Paula, his father's nurse who helps him the most. In this monologue, OZZY tells her that he wants his father to die and believes these thoughts have (deservedly) 'infected' him with cancer as well. The only way in which he can voice these feelings aloud is through the third person.

OZZY

Make it

Make it there's this guy. And this guy's dad is dying – everybody says so. And even though he never really got on with his dad he goes to the hospital every day. Because that's what you do.

And he even tells people that he's trying to help his dad. He tells people…he tells this one person, that he's making up stories in the hope that these stories will bring him back to life. His dad was a writer see. This guy's not a writer. This guy's nothing. But he tells her that he hopes the stories will help.

But it wasn't really true. In his heart…

See. In his heart he hopes the dad'll die. Because it's awful living with him. The fact that his dad is dying makes living – just simple day to day living – impossible. And he can't stand it anymore.

So he wishes him away. Secretly. Whisper, whispered it, in his heart. And he tells the stories because he knows his dad will hate it. Absolutely hate it. He'll hate hearing every dumb word coming from this guy's mouth. And the wish is, that he'll hate it so much that eventually he'll give up and go.

But that wish, that tiny black, bad, bad, wish, can't stay hidden. It can't. It grows into a heart where the whole world can see it. A broken heart. And that broken heart slowly fills with his dad's cancer.

He takes the cancer from his father. Takes the death from him. That's what he gets. And it serves him right.

This guy's had it coming.

I AM THE WIND

by Jon Fosse

*(English-language version
by Simon Stephens)*

Simon Stephen's version of Jon Fosse's play I Am the Wind *was
first performed at the Young Vic, London, in May 2011.*

Two men are out at sea on a boat trip. 'The One' is a competent
sailor but is depressed about his life. 'THE OTHER' has never
been on a boat before and is a little nervous when they head
out to open sea. When The One stumbles overboard, he refuses
THE OTHER's attempts to save him. Now THE OTHER is left
alone on a boat he does not know how to sail, steer or navigate.

THE OTHER

Don't stand there
Come on
No don't do that
Come back
The waves are getting really big
Come back
I'm scared
Quite short pause
I don't want to steer the boat
You
take the boat
Quite short pause
Come back
Be careful
Please come back

...

And then he stood there on the deck
He stood there and looked
quite short pause
and then
quite short pause
right then
then he sort of stumbled
quite short pause
and then he lay there in the sea
quite short pause
and I grabbed a life jacket
and I threw it to him
and the waves were huge

quite short pause
but he didn't reach for it
quite short pause
and the waves rolled over him
quite short pause
he was above the waves
quite short pause
he was under the waves
quite short pause
he lay there in the water
and the waves were getting bigger
quite short pause
I grabbed the boathook
I tried to reach him
I tried to get hold of him
but he pushed the boathook away
quite short pause
he was above the waves
quite short pause
he was under the waves
quite short pause
and then I saw him drift away behind the boat
quite short pause
and I
quite short pause
I had never sailed a boat before
I didn't know anything
In the middle of the ocean
the boat just drifts
the sails flapping

what am I meant to do
I pushed the tiller
nothing happened
the boat just kept drifting
and then
suddenly
the boat drifts forwards
but where is he
I look for him
I shout
where are you
he's nowhere to be seen
I've got to find him
I've got to get hold of him
the boat drifts forwards
I push the tiller
the boat stops
the sails flap
the boat lies there
and then it drifts backwards
and I look for him
I shout out
Where are you
the boat calms down
the sails flutter
I push the tiller
the boat drifts forwards
I look for him and look for him
I shout
Where are you

I shout again
Where are you
I look
The boat drifts forwards
I look and look
I push the tiller
The boat drifts forwards
I look and look
But I can't see him

...

I shout out
Where are you
The boat drifts forwards
I shout out
Where are you
The boat drifts forwards
I wait
I shout out
Where are you

...

I wait
The boat drifts forwards
I push the tiller
The boat drifts forwards
I've got to do something
Long pause
I look out over the water
quite short pause
and all I can see
is the open ocean

Everything's empty
Just ocean
Just sky
Just empty

THE KREUTZER SONATA
by Leo Tolstoy, adapted for the stage by Nancy Harris

This play was first performed at the Gate Theatre, London on 5 November 2009.

Adapted from a novella by Leo Tolstoy, *The Kreutzer Sonata* tells the story of how one man's jealousy led to the murder of his wife. POZDYNYSHEV is on a train after being released from prison. He reminisces about the events that led him to committing his terrible crime.

POZDYNYSHEV

After several hours, our conversation reached its natural
ebb and so I walked him to the door to bid our farewells.
And there it might have ended. Just like that. Two old
acquaintances catching up one morning – never to be in one
another's company again, but something – some devil inside
of me decided to reach out and I found myself saying, 'Wait,
no. You mustn't go yet. You haven't even had the pleasure of
meeting my wife.'

Beat.

It only took him a moment. She had just come in from her
morning walk and arrived at the study in her coat, her –
purple scarf thrown around her shoulders, her hair a little
wild form the wind, but she looked nothing short of – breath-
taking. Trukhachevski took a step backwards when he saw her,
almost stumbled. Not what he'd expected, clearly. Well. Not
from a man like me.

I saw his eyes brighten as he introduced himself. Hers lower
as she muttered her 'hellos.' Then they looked up and for a
time, that seemed, to me, to last for several hours, they took
each other in.

Perhaps he lights another cigarette. Lets this sink in.

Had they been beasts in a forest there is nothing surer than
they would have been rutting right there. I know men. I knew
my wife. I saw the invitation.

She broke their gaze first, Trukhachevski quickly followed
suit. She took on a look of the utmost sincerity and began

to ask questions of the most banal kind. Where did he live? How long was he staying? Had he many people to visit? He answered pleasantly, politely, even – glanced for my approval at moments. Eventually I lost patience. 'The two of you have much more in common than you realise,' I said. 'My wife is a musician too.'

His interest was immediately aroused. Didn't take a minute to extend his offer. He would be happy to accompany her playing, any day that suited while he was still in town. My wife blushed right up to her eyelids. Stuttered and stammered and called herself a novice, not nearly good enough. 'Nonsense,' I said. 'You must play with him.' And I invited him for dinner that night.

He sits back allowing this to settle.

At court, it was asked if I planned it. Or – or if I set the whole thing up as a test? Well, I couldn't have said this to a judge of course, but the only possible answer was…what was there to test? When you know who a person is, you know what they're capable of. You know their interests and desires and just how far they'll go – you know what attracts them and you know what bores them and after a while…it's you.

BEHOLD THE COACH, IN A BLAZER, UNINSURED

by Will Eno

This monologue was first performed as part of Oh, the Humanity and other good intentions *at the Flea Theater, New York on 3 November 2007.*

THE COACH of an unknown sport holds an uncomfortable press conference where he must explain his team's failure to win any games.

THE COACH

He enters, places his keys, cigarettes etc. on the table. Sits down.

All right, everybody, let's just get going. You people know what I've come here to probably say. This should all come as no surprise. The phrase, of course, you are familiar with. It was a 'building year,' this last year was. We suffered some losses, yes, we suffered some, last season, and we had to start out all over, in a fashion; we had to come at this thing as if it were a – you folks in the press can tell me if this is a pleonasm – a new beginning. We made some changes here and there and here and we made these, mainly, mostly, with the fans in mind, because we wanted the fans to be happy, in our minds we wanted the fans to love us. And I think they should be happy, in my mind I think they should love us.

Listen, last year was not the easiest year. The plan was that it would be for building, for rebuilding, for replacing what was lost, replenishing what was gone, and trying to reverse a routine of losing that had grown in-grown and somehow strangely proud. Our strategy was, in theory, to betray that which has become merely habit, to betray our very fear, the very thing that's kept us alive, the thing that says to us: Don't cross the street without looking both ways first; Don't speak your mind and certainly never your heart.

    Brief pause.

But habit's a hard habit to break.

    Brief pause.

And was it only habit that kept us from dropping to our knees in the middle of the street and sobbing and begging 'Can somebody help me, please?' Was it just mere routine that kept us on our feet, with our mouths shut and our hands in our pockets?

One night after practice – some of you might appreciate this – I found myself standing in the unforgivable light of a grocery store, staring at my reflection in a freezer, and realizing: 'You're not having a bad day – this is just what you look like, now. This is who the years are making you.' The praying kind probably would have prayed. I just wanted to grab a courtesy phone and beg into it: 'Could someone come to the front of the store and clean up the spill that is my life on this earth? Could somebody please just somehow help me through this punishing crushing nauseating sorrow?'

Brief pause.

So that's what this last year was. We had to look hard at a few things and, surprise surprise, we found that they looked hard back. But in many ways, I think we have to be happy. We sold some hot dogs. We got some sun, some fresh air. We played some close games – some of them, even, we were still in until right up to the end. It was the life, it really was, and, granted, yeah, no, this was not the greatest year. Some people are saying it was barely even a shambles. I'm sure there's a more charitable view, but, okay: fair enough. Fair enough.

PART FOUR: FORTIES PLUS

THIS OTHER CITY
by Daragh Carville

*This Other City was first performed in a production by
Tinderbox Theatre Company at the Baby Grand Opera House,
Belfast, on 30 April 2009.*

PATRICK is a well-groomed 40-year-old business man in
Belfast, who is husband to Gemma and father to fifteen-year-
old Orla. However, PATRICK has a secret: he likes having sex
with anonymous Eastern European prostitutes. This monologue
is set in a Belfast Hotel at the start of the play and he is trying
to justify his actions to the latest girl. It isn't long after this that
his family discovers his secret life and they are all forced to re-
evaluate their lives.

PATRICK

I'm a good man.

You have to know that, first of all, first and foremost, you have to understand that. I mean, I want you to know. This isn't – me.

Well, I mean, it is, I know that. But.

Look, I have a family. Let me tell you about my family. I have some pictures here actually. On my phone. *(Taking it out.)* They're not very good, but.

He puts the phone away.

You don't want to see my pictures. Nobody wants to see pictures of other people's families. You never know what to say, do you? Like holiday snaps. Or other people's dreams. No one gives a fuck. Why should they?

I'm the same. I'm the exact same.

Alright, lookit, start again. Rewind. Thing is, I have a daughter. Wee girl of my own. Orla. Well, I say wee girl. She's actually, I mean she's actually fifteen now. It's… But she's, she's such a great kid. I mean, I know all parents… But she is. She just is. She's smart, she's funny, she does well at school. She's – amazing. Sometimes I look at her and I just feel so much – I mean, this is embarrassing, but it's like I just feel so much love, it's like I can't breathe. And she'll catch me looking at her and she'll just smile. Her smile. And the way she smells. The top of her head. When she was wee.

And I'm a good man. Good father. I know I have to protect her. I mean, I know she's growing up and she's going to have to make her own way in the world, and the day will come when she has to go out there and, and stand on her own two feet. Out in the big bad world and. But I can't help it. It's like, that's my job. Y'know? I'm her dad and I have to protect her. From everything that's bad in the world. From all the bad people. Cos I know, I know what it's like out there. Believe you me. I've seen it all. The works.

Do you understand? Cos maybe your English…

It's just, I'm trying to explain this. Not because I have to, you understand. Because I want to.

I'm a good man. You understand me? I'm a good man.

Now come here. Come over here.

Because I want to fuck you in the skull.

BLUE HEART AFTERNOON
by Nigel Gearing

Blue Heart Afternoon *was first performed at Hampstead
Theatre, London, on 5 April 2012.*

It's Hollywood, 1951. The SONGWRITER (aka Ernie Case),
somewhere between 40 and 60 years old, already has an Oscar
for a hit song ('Blue Heart Afternoon') and an aspiring actress
in his bed. Now he has a new project with the Studio but he
must convince the Diva to take a part in it (as well as steer
clear of Senator McCarthy's anti-communist witch hunt). The
following speech is described as his 'party piece' and he uses it
to try and win the Diva over. However, despite what he says,
she later finds out that he grew up in a rich suburb in Buffalo.

SONGWRITER

I was raised in New York, right? Lower East Side. Five-, six-storey tenement buildings where the front stoop is always cracked and, well, you've seen 'em – inside the banisters are wobbly and the stairways ain't making no promises either… And here we lived: our family and hundreds of others just like us. And every parent or grandparent was – it seemed – an immigrant. And, of course, a Jew.

Come the summer, it'd get so hot first the kids then practically whole families would sleep out on the fire escape or the roof, like it was one huge dormitory. Only this old guy that lived under us – 'Mr Kosilowski' – would not sleep out. Rarely left the building at all. Spoke maybe fifty words of American and spent his entire days and evenings trying to get Europe on some home-made radio he'd cooked up.

So, one long summer evening this baby three floors above us starts screaming. From seven o'clock on, for hour after goddam hour. 'Meningitis', perhaps – who knows? But the mother can't be persuaded to either take him away or let go of him… First of all people try to 'understand'. A few of the younger ones start playing basketball down in the yard just to ignore it. Then the complaints begin. Some begin to get nasty, threaten to kill the baby <u>and</u> the mother both. But pretty soon everyone without exception is going kinda nuts…

And then, all of a sudden, crackling with static, going in and out of tune, is the sweetest music you ever heard.

He starts to play an appropriate music – austere but poignant. As he does so:

Mama said it was a tune 'from the Old Country'. Bullshit.
It was no such thing – it was a song-cycle by Schubert – this
I learned later – and it was old Kosilowski playing it on his
radio, the volume turned way up high… And now – the
damnedest thing – suddenly that baby isn't screaming
anymore and 'cos the <u>baby</u>'s gone quiet after all this time
so has everyone else – stopped talking, arguing, laughing,
cursing. Even the kids down in the yard have just gathered up
their ball and gone inside without a murmur… And still the
Schubert goes on and before you know it somehow the whole
block has gone to sleep for the night like they've taken a drug
or heard the greatest lullaby in the world.

Later I heard all manner of things – that the kid had died
that night, that on the contrary the kid recovered and grew
up to be a genius… To me it didn't matter. All I knew at
that moment was the peace, the silence, the <u>awe</u> that fell on
those people like showers of rain. I have only one word for it:
'religious'.

DEEP HEAT
by Robin Soans

Selections from Deep Heat *were first performed at a National Theatre Platform in London on 9 May 2011.*

Deep Heat, subtitled 'Encounters with the Famous, the Infamous and the Unknown', contains verbatim monologues collected and edited by Robin Soans. The following excerpt is the written voice of ALI BOYRAZ, a former member of the PKK (the Kurdish resistance movement) who now lives in East London. He was born in a Kurdish mountain village in South-East Turkey but his family were forced to move to the city when the Government removed subsidies to their community. He was drawn into the PKK in his teens and was eventually hunted down and imprisoned by the Turkish government. ALI was 43 years old when his experiences were recorded. This particular monologue is entitled 'The Free Man'. In it he talks about his injuries from prison, coping with life on his release and a chance encounter with one of his torturers.

ALI

My whole body is covered with scars...let me show you...
look where they tied my ankles...it's worn away a whole ring
of flesh, and look at these scars in my hair...this is where they
opened up the flesh with their batons and then shaved away
the loose flesh. And my feet are a strange shape...they used
to beat the soles of my feet with metal pipes...one particular
night they smashed my feet three times for not singing the
national anthem...I couldn't walk for two months.

But I believe I am strong mentally. If I wasn't I wouldn't
have lasted twenty-one years in jail. And I am aware of my
peculiarities...I greet them like old friends...sometimes they
make me smile. Even now, even tonight, on my way to here,
there was a football match at White Hart Lane, so there
were very few buses, but I couldn't bear to stand still and
wait for one, I had to keep walking...I can't bear standing
still. This is alright here, underground, but out in the street,
out in the open...I still feel hunted. I get angry about stupid
things...if someone throws litter in the street, I get unusually
angry...it's about order. I see people who don't have a plan
for tomorrow. I had to have a mental plan to survive from
day to day to day...even here...I have to have a plan to deal
with things. And the most shocking things happen out of the
blue. Let me tell you my friend. I was born in a tiny Kurdish
mountain village in the south-east of Turkey, not far from the
Iraqi border. In winter the snow was so deep, we had to dig a
tunnel to the well. I mean remote, and yet seventy per cent...
yeah I would say seventy percent of the people in that village
are now living in Hackney, Dalston or Tottenham. I work in

my uncle's newspaper shop next to Highbury and Islington Station...I unpack things and help behind the counter, and you know how busy it gets, specially in the morning and evening...and one day a fortnight ago, morning time...there is a queue, and we are serving, and busy, and...there is a laugh, from a man in the queue...he is talking in Turkish and laughing with his friends behind him, and he turns round to face the counter with this grin still on his face...and he does not know me, this man with the smile on his face, but it is a face I could never forget. The last time I saw him he was fitting electrodes to my testicles, and he had a magneto...you know this thing?... it is like an old wind-up gramophone...the faster you wind it the more the shock. This man was an expert...he would slow down and speed up to keep you on the edge of consciousness. The man next to me in that cell was having needles inserted into his balls, and the two guards were laughing and getting pleasure from inventing new ways of causing us pain. And now here he was in my uncle's shop laughing with his friends as he bought a packet of Drum rolling tobacco for his roll-ups.

THE RIOTS

by Gillian Slovo (from spoken evidence)

The Riots *was commissioned by Nicholas Kent at the Tricycle Theatre and was first performed there on 17 November 2011.*

This play was developed from spoken evidence collected by Gillian Slovo after the London riots that took place in the summer of 2011. MOHAMED HAMMOUDAN was living with his family in a flat above the Carpetright store in Tottenham that was set on fire by rioters in the middle of the night. He manages to escape with his two young children but loses everything he owns. In this monologue, he describes the events of that night.

MOHAMED HAMMOUDAN

As we got out the front door, I looked to my right and the place was ablaze. You could feel the heat coming through, yeah? You could feel the heat. I got my two boys over [the road] and as I was going across *(Breath.)* one of the neighbours said 'Could you take my son across as well?' Because they were tryna get some other people out of, of, of th-this stairwell you see? They were coughing, they couldn't get out. So I took him and waited and as I was waiting, I'm thinking the fire brigade are gonna come in a minute, yeah? The police are gonna be here in a minute. I was still thinking 'This is gonna be OK. Yeah, it's gonna be OK'. An' then it it kin- it kinda felt really unsafe because you've got your children there y- and you're y-y-you're f- you're kinda feeling really vulnerable, you haven't got your mobile phone, you haven't got – *(Breath.)* you haven't got your wallet, you haven't got *anything*. Everything you just left behind you an-an-and fleed out. And erm an'then you've got, you've got, it kinda felt really weird because you've got these people who're just out of the building looking at their their their homes being burnt up and then other people with a sense of euphoria going on. It felt like, it felt like our building was like a trophy.

…

I started talking to, to some of these young people. I said to 'em, 'This is not Aldis, this not McDonald's, this is not JD Sports, this is a residential area where people live.' Cos at the time other young people, where there was a erm wher- was a tyre shop nearby, yeah? Were throwing the tyres *in*to the fire t-to make it fuel even more. And one of these th-th-this young woman who's sitting in, in un-underneath a bus stop was saying to me 'Well you're just trying to prang me up?' Wh-which means you know tryna make you feel guilty. And then there was thi-thi-this this smiling lad erm who said 'Are you telling the truth? D-do people actually live in there?' I said 'Yes, people *are* living there above the shop. I'm gonna take you to other people who are just in the same situation as me and they're gonna say – tell you exactly the same thing' [and] he actually realised I am telling the truth. Yeah? And his immediate reaction was like 'This has gone too far. It weren't supposed to be like this.' *(Breath.)* An' I said to him 'What d'you mean? "It weren't supposed to be like this?"' He se-he se- he said 'It was supposed to be us and the police and the people who've been oppressing us'. So I said 'Who? Who's been oppressing you?' An' he said 'Well the government, y'ow? The government has been oppressing us'. And then, then, then he said, which is quite ironic, *(Laugh.)* 'e goes 'An I've gotta get up and fast tomorrow as well'. And I couldn't make out whether he was just a part of the looting and rioting or he actually was a part of setting the whole building a-alight.

THE PROPHET
by Hassan Abdulrazzak

The Prophet *received its UK premiere at the Gate Theatre,*
Notting Hill on 14 June 2012.

In 2011, Egypt erupted into revolution. Layla and Hisham, a
middle-class couple in their 30s, live in downtown Cairo. On
28 January, Layla (head engineer at a telecommunications
company) decides to join the revolutionary protest. However,
Hisham (a writer) chooses to attend a meeting with an important
literary agent instead. The agent takes him to an abandoned
building where he is tortured for a confession (as a student,
Hisham betrayed his best friend, Wael, to the authorities and
eventually married Wael's girlfriend, Layla). Later we learn that
the guilt-ridden Hisham only imagined his torture: in reality,
the agent cancelled the appointment. This monologue is spoken
by Hisham's invented torturer, METWALI. Even a torturer has
hobbies.

METWALI

I'm just here to loosen you up a bit. Open up those closed
channels to your brain. It's my job. It's what I do. And I'm
good at it. Because I take pride in it. It's not my passion
though. Do you want to know what my passion is? I mean
besides beautiful women.

Pause.

Well I'll tell you. Pigeons. *(Pause.)* What? You look surprised.
A man like me can't have such a hobby? Why not? This is
what you opposition figures never appreciate. My job is
stressful. Getting confessions out of people is very stressful.
My hobby helps me to deal with that stress. There is nothing
more relaxing after a hard day's work than to go back to my
apartment block and head straight to the roof.

METWALI speaks of his pigeons with great tenderness.

I keep my pigeons in a cage that I built with these two hands.
I feed them every day. Sometimes they get in a fight and
they'll have wounds that need attending to. I take care of
them as if they were my own children. I love those birds.
I love them. I've got around twenty now and I set them
free to soar high in the Cairo sky. Sometimes I imagine
where they go, I'm with them, I'm flying above the noise
and the pollution, above the garbage of my neighbourhood
and its filthy worn down pavements, soaring so high into
the air and who knows where they go, maybe as far as your
neighbourhood and the apartment block you live in with your
beautiful wife. You and I, we are not so different after all. We
live in the same city, breathe the same air. Similar thoughts,

good or bad, cross our minds. Yet there is one difference. You judge me. You give yourself the licence to judge me. I don't. I take you as you are.

SANCHO: AN ACT OF REMEMBRANCE

by Paterson Joseph

Sancho *was first performed at the Oxford Playhouse on 21 September 2011.*

CHARLES IGNATIUS SANCHO was born on a slave ship in 1729 to African parents who did not survive. He was taken to England and given as a 'gift' to three maiden sisters living in Greenwich. Eventually he was educated by the Duke of Montagu and ended up working as a servant, writer and actor. His portrait was painted by Thomas Gainsborough in the pose of a gentleman of the period. SANCHO is in his forties when the play opens and he reminisces (with the audience) about his life. In this excerpt, we learn how at seven he fell in love with acting and came to the attention of David Garrick, while taking part in a salon entertainment. He played the role of Sancho Panza, Don Quixote's servant.

SANCHO

I was some seven years into my life when my world was
suddenly lit as 'twere by a Fire-work and I was dazzled awake,
as when a sweet dream is ended abruptly. Every detail of
the moment is branded upon my brain – due to its mix of
joy…and violence, perhaps? It went thus… We had played
the scenes of Panza meeting his Don and their arrangements
concerning their long journey together etc., etc. And here we
were in Act Four.

*(He quickly grabs his cloak and cane, draping the former
over his shoulder and putting the cane between his legs like a
hobby horse. He is enjoying the memory immensely. Lighting
resembles a candle-lit stage.)*

My Quixote – already the worse for several glasses of port
and a very large supper, enters on his steed… *(Indicates
cane.)* a hobby horse from the nursery. *(To a woman in the
audience re: the cane.)* It wasn't *that* kind of play, madam…
A great cheer goes up from the gathered throng – Their hero
has entered yet again… He addresses me thus, *(As a boozy
old ham.)* 'Fortune is arranging matters for us better than we
could have shaped our desires ourselves, for look there, friend
Sancho Panza, where thirty or more monstrous giants present
themselves, all of whom I mean to engage in battle and slay.'
(Sweetly, shyly, as his seven-year-old self.) 'What giants?' –
quoth I. *(As Quixote.)* 'Those thou seest there, with the long
arms, and some have them nearly two leagues long.' *(Panza.)*
'Look, your worship, what we see there are not giants but…
Windmills…and what seem to be their arms are the sails that*

turned by the wind make the millstone go'. (Quixote.) 'It is
easy to see that thou art not used to this business of adventures;
those are giants; and if thou art afraid, away with thee out
of this and betake thyself to prayer while I engage them in
fierce and unequal combat.' And with that, he tangles himself
in a Gordian Knot of cloak, curtains – limbs and scenery...
And though crowd and actor laughed fit to die, myself felt it
keenly that he was mortal wounded. Genuine tears sprang to
my eye and *that* silenced both spectator and actor... *(Panza*
addressing the cane as if to Quixote in his arms.) 'God bless
me! Did I not tell your worship to mind what you were about,
for they were only windmills? And no one could have made any
mistake about it but one who had something of the same kind
in his head.' (Quixote, in earnest and to the cane as if to young
Sancho.) 'Hush, friend Sancho, the fortunes of war more than
any other are liable to frequent fluctuations.' (Panza.) 'God
order it as he may.'

(SANCHO takes a small bow.)

Well, the crowd erupted in genuine applause. Two strong
gentlemen lifted me on to their shoulders and paraded me
around that salon; transformed for me into the very stage at
Drury Lane – Its soon to be resident, Davy Garrick raised his
glass to me at that moment; though I was only afterwards told
who he was – My three guardians...were content to be the
centre of so much unexpected attention and compliments.
They had *bred* me well was the general opinion.

DANDY IN THE UNDERWORLD
by Tim Fountain

This play was first performed at Soho Theatre, London,
on 9 June 2010.

Dandy in the Underworld tells the story of SEBASTIAN
HORSLEY in his own words. He was an artist, writer and dandy
but also a hustler, class A drug user and lover of prostitutes, who
lived in London's Soho. 'Dandy in the Underworld' was the
title of SEBASTIAN's autobiography, taken from his favourite
Marc Bolan album. He died of a suspected overdose at 47 years
old only a few days after this play opened in the West End.

SEB

It is upon the parchment of Turnbull and Asser's sacred tomes that my great legacy is recorded: The Horsley shirt. Four button cuff. Five inch turn back. Collar point: five inches – wide enough to fly. But it will be the buttons I am remembered by – the covered buttons to be precise. There is something so rude about a naked button. I am the only male customer to have ever insisted upon covered fastenings for his shirt. I even had diamanté on the cuffs and engraved silver stays. Some dimwit once said 'There's no point' instantly reassuring me that was *precisely the point.* Hats of course are the crowning glory of a dandy. Beau Brummell and Byron went to Locks and so did I. Four fur fedoras. Fur felt, antelope velour, grosgrain band and bow with feather mount, satin lining and roan leather. Few things look more ridiculous than a hat on a man who doesn't suit hats and nothing looks more ridiculous than an ivory White fedora on a man who doesn't suit hats, which is why I wore one. I spent over £100,000 on my wardrobe. I simply had to squander oodles of money as fast as I hadn't earned it so as to escape the tortures of having to do something sensible with it. Once I had tired of a Huntsman special I would wear them as painting overalls. From Savile Row to B and Q with nothing in between. I think the drugs had a part to play in that. When I was using I didn't care about my clothes. I once sold £20,000 worth of suits for three hundred quid to a man from Billy Smart's circus who was re-costuming the clowns.

Looks out the window.

Talking of drugs the smack dealer's out on Meard Street. For some reason he still hangs around outside my door even though I haven't bought anything from him for an age. Heroin's like a whore who gave you the best fuck you ever had. She may have stolen your credit card and given you clap but a part of you always feels like going back for more. The fixing ritual is one of the sweetest pleasures known to man. The only problem is the dealers end up stealing your life. In the case of my last crack dealer, English – quite literally. It was hilarious. When he first came to me he drove a Nissan Micra and wore a baseball cap swiveled backwards. I used to say to him 'English, please if you are going to deliver me five hundred pounds of crack cocaine you could at least dress for the occasion'. But by the end of our time together he was driving a BMW and wearing smart suits and I was the one who looked like a tramp. Then to add insult to injury he took up art. He turned up one day and said 'I've got something for you'. I said 'I know – now give it to me'. But instead of spitting out a little cellophane package he unravelled some sketches he'd done. It was as if he'd gone to the fancy dress shop and asked for the Sebastian Horsley.

DEEP HEAT
by Robin Soans

Selections from Deep Heat *were first performed at a National Theatre Platform in London on 9 May 2011.*

Deep Heat, subtitled 'Encounters with the Famous, the Infamous and the Unknown', contains verbatim monologues collected and edited by Robin Soans. The following excerpt is the written voice of PHILIP, a 50-year-old actor who is understudying a principal role in a provincial theatre. We find him in the Green Room, while the play is in performance (faintly heard in the background over the tannoy). However, Simon, the principal actor, becomes ill during the performance and PHILIP is soon summoned onto the stage.

PHILIP

Eight across…Indian currency…five letters beginning with R…yes, well that's going to be rupee…and there you see… that gives you a P third in two down…P blank P…so it's poppy, thought it was, but I don't like to fill it in til I'm sure.

I take my understudy role very seriously as you can tell, and it is a responsible position. I know I don't get the glory, but they also serve who only stand and wait, and you never know when your hour will come, do you, and it's no good being thrust into the limelight half-cock, if you see what I mean. I sometimes think people don't realise the hard work that goes on under the surface. No one goes on 'krill watch' do they? 'Come on everyone, let's pack up a picnic and go and watch some krill.' But the truth is there wouldn't be any whales if there wasn't krill for them to feed on, and I don't know about you, but I don't think krill get the credit they deserve. Whether the audience realises it or not, the understudy is an insurance policy to make sure they get their evening's entertainment. Children at the circus can only really enjoy the trapeze artists, cos they know there's a safety net. You couldn't have some glitter-clad nymphette plummeting to her death every five minutes could you…and that's what I am…a safety net… and if anything happens to Simon…you know…laryngitis can attack the greatest…or if in mid-performance he gets a peanut stuck in his windpipe, or he trips over a stage brace and concusses himself on the sideboard…there I am to seamlessly take up the mantle, and carry the audience safely through to Curtain Down.

Then again, this is only part of my work. I am an actor in my own right. I've been head juror on *Crown Court*, I was the man across the street in *One Foot in the Grave*...I got a good laugh on that. I had my head chopped off in a thing about The Plantagenets...I was a delivery man in *Upstairs Downstairs*. I nearly hit the jackpot last year...I got down to the last two for that *Specsavers* advert where the man and his wife sit down to eat a cheese sandwich...and actually they sit down on a roller coaster thing and go whizzing about all over the place...funnily enough a friend of mine got that part and I thought he did it very well, so I wasn't that upset about it.

There's something not quite right...listen...that's not Simon and Gillian...listen...

Sebastian Faulk's
BIRDSONG
in a stage version by Rachel Wagstaff

Birdsong *was first performed at the Comedy Theatre, London on 18 September 2010, produced by Creative Management and Productions (CMP), Becky Barber Productions and ACT Productions.*

Based on Sebastian Faulk's international best-selling novel, *Birdsong* follows Stephen Wraysford's experiences in France prior to and during the First World War. This speech takes place in 1916 at the front line of the Somme. COLONEL BARCLAY is Wraysford's commanding officer and gives final instruction to the junior officers and foot soldiers before they 'go over the top' of the trenches to attack the German line. He maintains an unfailing belief that the English will triumph despite the difficult circumstances. But, ultimately, the initial bombardment does not destroy German defences and the men are required to walk in daylight to their slaughter.

COLONEL BARCLAY

For those of you who don't know, I am Colonel Barclay,
and it's a pleasure to be leading such a fine and upstanding
collection of men. I'm sure you all know why we're here, in
this splendid village of Auchonvillers, in the valley of the River
Somme. Now then, you'll be relieved to hear that we're about
to attack. Tomorrow, we will inflict a defeat on the Boche such
that he will never recover... Of course I'll be in the trench
and going over with you chaps. Aiming to have dinner off the
regimental silver in Bapaume. Over at dawn, we punch a hole,
the cavalry pour through. That reminds me. The sappers'll
blow the ridge as we go. No, before we go. Yes, that's right. To
recap. The sappers blow their mines, we go over, a nice steady
trot – try to hold your lines, nothing worse than a scrappy
advance, regroup at midday, take a breather if necessary, then
shoulder to the wheel and we'll be through by early evening.
As you know, we've just dished out a six-day bombardment
that'll have cut every bit of German wire from here to Dar-
es-Salaam. If there's any Boche left alive he'll be so bloody
relieved it's over, he'll come out with his hands in the air. Well
then. Gentlemen, good luck.

A cheer starts –

Oh yes, one last thing. I need hardly remind you of the
glorious history of this regiment. I can say no more to
you than this: I believe from the bottom of my heart that
tomorrow you will live up to our mighty nickname, that of
'The Goats'. God bless you all and see you in Bapaume!

A cheer is raised.

LULLABIES OF BROADMOOR: WILDERNESS

by Steve Hennessy

Wilderness *is one of four plays published under the title of* Lullabies of Broadmoor *and was first produced by Theatre West in October 2002.*

All four plays in *Lullabies of Broadmoor* are based on true stories of Broadmoor inmates during the late nineteenth and early twentieth centuries. *Wilderness* focuses on DR WILLIAM CHESTER MINOR, who had been a surgeon in the Union Army during the American Civil War. He was traumatised by the experience and soon after arriving in London he shot and killed George Merrett, a furnace stoker at the local brewery who was walking home after shift work. MINOR was delusional, thinking that Merrett had tried to break into his lodgings. Soon after, MINOR was committed to the Broadmoor asylum where he remained for 38 years. Merrett's widow, Eliza, visited him, bringing papers and books for his research (he submitted entries for the Oxford English Dictionary from Broadmoor). In the following monologue, MINOR is alone in his cell, reminiscing about his experiences in the American Civil War.

DR MINOR

Winter rains uncovered the skeletons of men who died in the previous year's battle. Two soldiers played catch with a skull. I begged respect for our fallen comrade. They laughed in my face, smashed the skull against a rock until it shattered.

We crossed Virginia into a region named 'The Wilderness', seventy square miles of hardwood trees. From the rocky heights overlooking it, green virgin forest as far as the eye could see, as if the hand of God had just made it. And very rugged – thick underbrush, ravines, few clearings except for pockets of swamp. As if Nature was trying to create one place we could not dump the filth of war. She failed.

(Distant sounds of gunfire, artillery, men's cries.)

Never this close to battle before. Men fight their way through brambles and thorns as artillery shells and explosive bullets rip them to pieces. Trees hung with human flesh drip blood on those who struggle beneath. Fires sweep through the dry brush. Our dressing stations overwhelmed; the most terrible injuries. Men blackened, burned beyond recognition, with shattered limbs and holes through their bodies who will never survive. Clawing me with sooty fingernails. 'Don't let me die, doctor! Save me…'

Twenty-seven thousand die in two days, countless more maimed in body and mind. What do *I* do? Report the two soldiers I saw smashing the skull. 'I have *slightly* more important matters to worry about,' the senior officer drawls, a cigarette hanging from his mouth. I persist, and without looking up from his desk he says, 'Dr. Minor. Go to hell.'

(Lights change to red. Smoke drifts across stage. Battle noises louder from this point, eventually MINOR will have to shout to be heard. Walls of cell start bulging inwards in several places as if people are trying to break in. Fire glows brighter, redder.)

Many wounded lie out in the undergrowth, unable to crawl back to their lines, choking on the smoke…roasted alive. After the screams stop… POP! POP! Unused rifle cartridges in their belts going off in the heat. POP! A cheerful sound. Like firecrackers on the fourth of July.

Forty-eight hours awake, sawing off limbs and still a queue of men on stretchers waits to go under my knife. Trees by the field hospital catch fire. Smoke pours in, and sparks rain down on us. I look up and see soldiers advancing, like devils through the flames. Our men or theirs? I no longer care. We have turned a primeval garden into Dante's 'Inferno'. How can it ever be turned back?

On that day I fix an opinion. Despite all our culture, books, music and everything noble that humankind has ever achieved, this earth would be a better place if we had never existed.

COLDER THAN HERE
by Laura Wade

*This play was first performed at Soho Theatre in London
on 3 February 2005.*

ALEC is 56 and his wife, Myra, is dying from cancer. She keeps
herself occupied by planning her own funeral and the cardboard
coffin that she has chosen sits in the middle of their living
room. ALEC and his two children, Harriet (29) and Jenna (27)
are not coping very well with the thought of a future without
their wife/mother. It is Myra who holds the family together. In
the midst of this turmoil, the boiler has broken and the house
is freezing. ALEC has been trying to get it fixed with limited
success.

ALEC

The reference number at the *bottom* of the page? ...
LS23161701... Mr A. Bradley, 26 Morris Avenue, look you
know who I am we've been on the phone all bloody week...

Right. I've got a letter in my hand saying you were going to
come round today and sort it out... Oh yes, someone came,
someone came and scratched his head at it, had a cup of tea,
said he couldn't fix it and toddled off again. Which to be
honest isn't what I had in mind.

Listen, mate – I'm sorry, do you mind if I call you mate, it's
not a word I'd normally use, but I feel we've spent a lot of
time together now... Richard. Right. Richard. Richard, when
are you going to fix my boiler?... Alright, try again: when –
specifically, in *time* – are you going to fix my boiler?

...Mmmm, uh huh... Do you know I have never encountered
incompetence on this level before? My daughter has this thing
she says (she's twenty-seven she talks like a teenager) the
thing she keeps saying is 'next level', everything's next-level
wrong, next-level horrid, next-level stupid. Well this is next-
level farcical if that's not a tautology.

...*Tautology*. It means – It doesn't matter... Could you just–
could you *let* me complain at you, I'm afraid I won't feel
complete until I've ruined your day too. I mean what is the
point, what is the blasted point of making a boiler so high-tech
there's only two chaps in the country can fix it? What is the
bloody point?... So if you agree why can't you do something
about it? Somebody somewhere in your company has to take
responsibility –

How many people where you're working, Richard? …How many can you see? …Where are you?… Good God, no wonder you don't care about my problems if you're in *Glasgow*.

Right, so I'm imagining, if the world's a fair place, that the others are spending a good portion of their time being screamed at by someone like me I mean I can't believe I'm completely alone in this… So what if you get everyone together and count up the amount of time you've spent listening to complaints about the CH 2010, which incidentally isn't the year you're going to fix my boiler in, and then you might work out there's a health and safety issue, something about stress and eardrums and you can all take your headpieces off and go over and tell the supervisor and maybe if you all club together and do something about it you might have the –

Hmm.

ALEC stops. He takes his glasses off and rubs his eyes.

No that's crap. Don't have the power to do anything, do you?

ALEC paces around the coffin, looking at it.

We've been cold for four months. You know how cold a house gets after that long? Nothing residual left.

Tell you something else – my wife is dying… No – no, it's not your fault. …Cancer. Bone cancer… No, she's going to die.

So you can imagine how this is making me weary. I am spending precious hours of her dwindling life talking to you. She wants to stay at home, she doesn't want to die in hospital, she wants to die at home, which between you and me I think is a drastically bad idea, but that's what she wants and by Christ I'll get it for her if I have to come to Glasgow and do the bloody training course myself.

…No, I'm a. I'm a chartered surveyor… No we don't do heating systems.

…Look, what it boils down to, excuse the pun, in essence what I'm saying here is the least you can do is let her die in the *warm*. It's bafflingly little to ask.

ALEC stands in the coffin.

…When? …DID YOU NOT HEAR A WORD I SAID? I want someone out here tomorrow, Richard. Tomorrow morning.

…Yes, Thursday should be fine. Yes, two o'clock.

ALEC hangs up the phone. He takes a breath.

Thursday.

RED
by John Logan

Red *was first performed at the Donmar Warehouse,
London on 3 December 2009.*

MARK ROTHKO is the Russian-born American painter, who
created abstract expressionist art in the twentieth century. *Red*
is set in ROTHKO's New York studio during the late 1950s
(when he was in his late 50s). He is working on a series of large
canvasses, commissioned by the architect/designers of the new
Seagram Building on Park Avenue. In this monologue, he tells
his young assistant, Ken, about his visit to the restaurant where
his work will hang.

ROTHKO

(*Reliving it.*) You go in from 52nd... Then you go up some stairs to the restaurant... You *hear* the room before you see it. Glasses clinking, silverware, voices, hushed here but building as you get closer, it's a desperate sound, like forced gaiety at gunpoint... You go in, feel underdressed, feel fat, feel too goddam Jewish for this place. Give your name. Pretty hostess gives you a look that says: 'I know who you are and I'm not impressed, we get millionaires in here, pal, for all I care you might as well be some schmuck painting marionettes in Tijuana.' She snaps for the Maitre D' who snaps for the captain who snaps for the head waiter who brings you through the crowd to your table, heads turning, everyone looking at everyone else all the time, like predators – who are you? what are you worth? do I need to fear you? do I need to acquire you?... Wine guy comes, speaks French, you feel inadequate, you obviously don't understand, he doesn't care. You embarrass yourself ordering something expensive to impress the wine guy. He goes, unimpressed. You look around. Everyone else seems to belong here: men with elegant silver hair and women with capes and gloves. Someone else in a uniform brings you the menu. It's things you never heard of: suckling pig under glass, quail eggs in aspic. You are lost. And then...you can't help it, you start hearing what people are saying around you... Which is the worst of all...

ROTHKO *pulls himself up.*

He stands there, unsteady. It's disquieting: the dripping red paint really does look like blood.

ROTHKO: The voices… It's the chatter of monkeys and the barking of jackals. It's not human… And everyone's clever and everyone's laughing and everyone's investing in this or that and everyone's on this charity board or that and everyone's jetting off here or there and no one looks at anything and no one thinks about anything and all they do is chatter and bark and eat and the knives and forks click and clack and the words cut and the teeth snap and snarl.

Beat.

He spreads his arms, taking in his murals:

ROTHKO: And in that place – *there* – will live my paintings for all time.

Beat.

He finally turns to KEN.

ROTHKO: I wonder… Do you think they'll ever forgive me?

MUSWELL HILL
by Torben Betts

This play was first performed at the Orange Tree Theatre, Richmond, on 8 February 2012.

TONY has turned up (unexpectedly) to a dinner party held by Mat and Jess at their fashionably decorated home in Muswell Hill. Also present are Karen, who is Jess's slightly-depressed single friend; Simon, an old university friend of Mat's, also single; and, Annie, Jess's younger sister. Annie (23) and TONY (60) are having an affair: in fact, Annie believes they are engaged (although TONY is already married with grown children). He works in a drama school and seduced Annie with the idea that she could become an actress. He tries to explain to Mat in the kitchen whilst drinking a rather large glass of wine.

TONY

…my main problem in this life, twixt thee and me, is that I'm surrounded by all this magnificent totty all day long. All wanting to be famous, all wanting to be somebody. All competing for my attention. And they seem to see me as the man who's going to help them. Who's going to open up the world to them. It's really quite hard to resist. I actually made an effort to stop indulging a while back because, well, it's never free, is it, and I was starting to find all the aggravation afterwards a bit…well, aggravating. But then you get to know them and then you fall for them a bit and they sort of represent a future you can never have, a life you can never know. Or hold. It's bloody murder really. But, you see, my wife's getting to be so… Belinda used to be quite a looker but now all she does is sit about the house, badgering our daughters to start breeding and, for God's sake, I'm not ready for all of that yet. I want to live. To keep tasting life. But the thing with Annie, what's happened with Annie and me is just so… Belinda went through my bloody text messages and… That was it. *(Upper crust.)* 'Mr Shit, I wonder if I might possibly introduce you to Mr Fan?' *(He laughs.)* So…anyway I'm holed up in a hotel room now. *(He drinks.)* And the thing is: not everyone can be successful. Can they? For every one successful person, you need to have about a thousand failures. But you never hear about all the people who fail. Do you? You only ever hear about the very few who actually make a bloody living at it.

THE GODS WEEP
by Dennis Kelly

The Gods Weep *was first performed by the Royal Shakespeare Company at Hampstead Theatre, London on 12 March 2010.*

Over the past thirty years COLM has built his empire: a vast company with subsidiaries in manufacturing, transport, security and petro-chemical research. Success has required ruthlessness and cruelty. However, now he is ready to relinquish some control by dividing and evolving power to two younger members of the board. Their subsequent power struggle is brutal and bloody with far-reaching consequences across the world that COLM created. This monologue takes place not long after COLM has handed over the bulk of his company to Richard and Catherine and the cracks have started to appear. He is speaking to his right-hand man, Castile, in a rare moment of self-revelation.

COLM

Last night I'm sitting there having dinner with my wife.
And we're not speaking. Not in a bad way. Not in a 'I've got
nothing to say to you, pass the salt' sort of way but in a loving
silence, a warm silence. So I'm sitting there having dinner
with my wife in a warm silence. I think it was lamb. And I
said 'Is this lamb?' and she said 'Yes. It's lamb. Don't you
like it?' and I said 'Yes. I think I like it.' And she said 'Think?
You think you like it?' and I said 'Yes. I think I like it' and she
said 'Shall I tell Angelina to make you something else?' and
I said 'Why would you do that when I think I like it? Isn't
that a positive?' and she said 'No, that's not a positive. Not if
you think you like something. It's only a positive if you like
something.' And I said 'Well what about us? I think I like you,
yet we've been married for twenty-five years.' And there was
a…catch, in her being, a microsecond of shock. And I thought
'Oh Christ, I've done it now' and I didn't mean to, Castile, I
really didn't, I just thought this was a given, but she's always
had remarkable powers of recovery and we just carried on, we
just carried on talking.

And we carry on eating. And there are silences, yes. But
comfortable silences. The silences of deep understanding.
And we're chatting, and she's telling me about her brother
and there's no hint of what was said, so much so that I'm
beginning to think that it never really happened and then,
then in the middle of a sentence, she looks up at me and says
'What do you mean "think"? What does "think" mean?'

Beat.

And I looked at her. And I saw in her face that one word from me, and she would collapse behind that smile. And I thought 'God, don't say the wrong thing' but I found myself saying 'Well, on the way home I almost asked Mario to drop me off at a brothel so I could pay a prostitute to let me fuck her in the mouth.'

…

And she looked…so surprised. And I said, 'Look, I'm saying this because I want to be honest, don't you want to be honest? I think I love you, I think I've loved you for twenty five years, isn't that enough? Please don't tell me that that isn't enough.'

And for a second, for a fraction of a second I thought 'Here we go. Here it comes, the eruption, she's going to explode…'

And she looked at me and opened her mouth and said 'You're in a funny mood tonight.' And then went back to the lamb.

Beat.

'You're in a funny mood tonight.'

And suddenly it occurred to me, Castile, that we had in fact been sitting in a 'pass the salt' sort of silence. That we had been sitting in that sort of silence for twenty five years. And I cried. I cried my lungs out. Inside. I cried my lungs out inside. Outside I just carried on eating the lamb.

I, SHAKESPEARE
by Tim Crouch

I, Shakespeare *was first performed at Dorothy Stringer High School, Brighton on 5 May 2010.*

Tim Crouch allows five of Shakespeare's lesser-known characters to have their say: MALVOLIO from *Twelfth Night*, Cinna the poet from *Julius Caesar*, Banquo from *Macbeth*, Caliban from *The Tempest* and Peaseblossom from *A Midsummer Night's Dream*. In *I, Malvolio*, MALVOLIO is feeling very sorry for himself after being the butt of so many jokes. He contemplates hanging himself and speaks directly to the audience.

MALVOLIO

It's all too easy, isn't it? To laugh at people. To let yourselves go. To exploit a weakness. To destroy the thing you're too lazy to take time to understand. To take pleasure in someone else's downfall.

The practical joke. Is that how it goes with you, is it? Is that what you do?

The bully?

With my lady grieving, with the madness taking hold. Toby Belch targets me. In effect, you target me. With your slouched shoulders and your stinking breath. You trick me. You bully me. Because you don't approve of the way I live my life. You don't approve of the way I look, the way I think.

Toby Belch gets his drunken friends together and they work up a plot that will bring me down. It's the easy option. The lazy option. A practical joke. Oh ha ha! Won't that be funny? One of many fruitless pranks this ruffian hath botched up.

Toby Belch encourages my lady's maiden to write a letter.

That letter.

He points to the letter on the floor.

A letter that looks like it's been written by my lady Olivia – in her very Cs and Us and her Ts. And her great Ps. A letter that is left for me to find. A letter declaring my lady's LOVE for me. For me! Her love for me her love for me her love for me (I were better love a dream).

He picks up the letter and reads from it.

'She thus advises thee that sighs for thee. Remember who commended thy yellow stockings and wished to see thee ever cross-gartered: I say, remember. Go to, thou are made, if thou desir'st to be so.'

'If thou entertain'st my love', it says, 'let it appear in thy smiling, thy smiles become thee well.'

A letter declaring my lady's desire to see me smile. A thing that I am not naturally inclined to do. To see me in yellow stockings with crossed garters. To see me 'surly with servants'. All of which things I do. Because for the first time, for the first time in my life, I think, I think, I think that somebody loves me and that I AM IN LOVE.

Not mad, but in love.

I AM IN LOVE. For the first time in my life. I am happy.

I AM HAPPY.

To be Count Malvolio!

What weakness. What glorious weakness. Love and happiness. Have you ever felt that? How ridiculous. For the first time I let my happiness in. AND I SMILE. *(He smiles.)* And I breathe and I FEEL! Sensuous. Physical. As a gentleman does towards a lady. Alive for the first time. Complete for the first time! Possible for the first time. I smile and I smile and I smile because that is what I think my lady wants. My body becomes alive to my lady. The thought of her touch!

Oh!

A paroxysm of smiles.

And look what happens. Look where it leads me.

The behaviour I believe is so desired by my lady becomes my downfall. My smiles are taken for lunacy. My yellow stockings are ridiculed for madness. I am accused of insanity and thrown in a cell where I am tormented and despised.

OBEDIENTLY YOURS, ORSON WELLES

by Richard France

from *Hollywood Legends: 'Live' on Stage*

This play was first performed as Votre Serviteur, Orson Welles
at the Theatre Marigny, Paris on 6 September 2006.

It is 1985 and ORSON WELLES has just turned 70. He sits in
a dingy LA recording studio with Mel, a sound engineer, who
is due to record his latest series of voice overs. WELLES' voice
is no longer what it once was and Mel is forced to 'enhance'
the recordings so that audiences will recognise his previous
distinctive style. Most importantly, WELLES is waiting to hear
if Spielberg will help finance the final edit of his unfinished
film, *Don Quixote*. The time is filled with reminiscences of his
life in the industry: sometimes he addresses Mel, sometimes
the microphone and sometimes even the theatre audience in
front of him.

WELLES

No studio would back me. I couldn't even get a loan from the bank. Unless you're a Spielberg or a Lucas, you can expect to spend more time putting the deal together than you will making the movie. College boys from NYU or USC or AFI! They sit around their boardrooms and speak in code. Points. Market share. Feasibility analysis. Snot-nosed little shits! It used to be... *(As if speaking on the phone.)* Orson Welles for Darryl Zanuck, please. *(To audience.)* He used to put me through my dancing bear routine, but in the end... *(On the phone; very effusive.)* Darryl! What a joy it is to hear a friendly voice for a change! *(Listens.)* I have all these people over here yelling at me – in Italian, no less. There's this little matter of a hotel bill I've run up. *(Listens.)* Yes, they're still with me, the whole company on full pension. *(Listens.)* If I do that, I can't be sure of getting them back when I need them. And if I'm ever going to finish this picture, I'd damned well... *(Listens.)* Don't you think I haven't already thought of that? *(Pouring it on.)* The *Carabinieri* are getting ready to storm the hotel. And the only other way out of here is to jump in the canal. *(Falls to his knees; playfully.)* Darryl, please! I'm on my knees to you. Save us! No-one else can. It's you or... *(His voice cracking.)* a watery grave. *(Thoroughly enjoying this shared pretence.)* You wouldn't want that on your conscience, would you?

(He nods confidently to the audience, gets to his feet, and takes a puff or two on his cigar.)

A hundred thousand should save the day. *(Listens.)* You still want me for *The Black Rose*, don't you? What do you think that's going to cost you? *(Listens.)* Good! Have your man wire the money to me here at the Colombe d'Or. Bye, Darryl! Bye, now!

(The lights change back, as he returns to the studio and sits down.)

Don't get the wrong idea: they were all monsters…the Zanucks…the Warners…the Harry Cohns. But they were also devoted to this business. Sam Goldwyn invited me onto the set of *Wuthering Heights*, and I said something like, 'What a good film Willie Wyler's making.' Goldwyn turned on me: '*I'm* making *Wuthering Heights*. Wyler's only directing it.' *(A more somber reflection.)* There's none of that spirit anymore. I'm not even sure Hollywood deserves to be called a movie town anymore. Maybe the industry's exhausted itself. When I was starting out, colour was all the rage. *(Mischievously.)* Of course, I ignored it. *(To his target in the audience.)* That surprises you? *(To everyone else.)* Are there any mavericks in the audience? *(Finds one.)* Acquaint him with our breed would you please? *(Back to his story.)* Then they came up with Cinerama… or CinemaScope. Now, everyone is worshipping at the altar of computer graphics. But through it all, what has mattered most to the audience? In my day all they cared about was whether Veronica Lake's hair was all her own – the same question that's asked today of Burt Reynolds. *(His devilish smile.)* The answer is yes…and no. Which is which? My lips are sealed. *(Again serious.)* I hope this doesn't sound like sour grapes. Hollywood is Hollywood. Whatever your luck – and I've had the very best luck, and the very worst luck, no-one forces you to sit down and join the game, so none of us has the right to be bitter. *(Puffs thoughtfully.)* I was merely…questioning the wisdom of my decision.

KALASHNIKOV:
IN THE WOODS BY THE LAKE
by Fraser Grace

The first performance of Kalashnikov *was at the Burton Taylor
Studio, Oxford Playhouse on 6 October 2011.*

The retired GENERAL KALASHNIKOV is classified as a
Soviet Hero for his invention of the AK-47. However, now he
is a frail, old man and lives in a dacha on the wild and frozen
outskirts of Izhevsk in the Russian Republic of Udmurtia with
his daughter, Makka, and granddaughter, Elena. He receives
a visit from a journalist, Volkov, who starts out recording the
GENERAL's personal history but soon confronts him with the
brutal atrocities in which his invention has been used. The
following monologue is taken from the opening scene of the
play, before Volkov arrives, and the GENERAL is proud to
present to the audience what he considers to be his greatest
achievement.

KALASHNIKOV

I am General Mikhail Timofeyevich Kalashnikov –
Retired. Semi-retired, I live here by the lake.
Across the water,
the other side of that great mirror
within sight, within sound almost,
lies my darling – Izhmash:
the most beautiful Motor Factory in all the Russias.
You smile; good!
It's good to smile!
That factory, Izhmash – she is the nest,
the womb from which my baby
– my modest achievement in the field of engineering –
took off round the globe,
K for 'Kalashnikov'
stamped on every little arse.

India, Africa, the Central Asian Republics
places I'd never been,
never dreamed I'd be allowed to travel to.

Coca Cola, Nike, BMW…Kalashnikov;
Everywhere my name goes before me.
Without me, these days.

He lights up.

Motor factory.
Another joke from the Soviet era.
We never built one tractor, one car

in our part of the factory
not even one of your Toyotas!
Guns, since 1809 –
Since 1947, the Kalashnikov assault rifle
Avtomat Kalashnikova
AK-47 – d'you see?
…
Child's play.
A child can dismantle and reassemble my gun
in under two minutes.
Unless the child's an idiot.
…
Now, pay attention.
I'm showing you what, if I may say, is the genius of our
design. You see?
Just a handful of parts, but
even when assembled,
everything has its own space –
room is given around the parts,
'As if each component
was suspended in air'
Dirt has nowhere left to lodge –
dust, ice, not a hope –
'The gun that keeps on firing'.
Unlike if I may say the gun
designed by my rival and eventual friend
in America, Mr Eugene Stoner:
The United States Army's M-16.
A fine man, Stoner, a gentleman, and a
good designer, but the M-16 in my opinion…

Well, in our tank unit we had a saying:

If it can rain, it will. So please, for the love of Stalin,

give us a gun that'll work when it's pissing down.

Besides

no one's going to put a weapon as ugly as the M-16 on

a t-shirt

much less a flag.

Eugene Stoner. Gone now,

like all the rest.

They do the AK you know. Put it on flags,

T-shirts too.

Who'd have thought –

Little Misha Kalashnikov – enemy of the people,

doyen of the fashion industry.

The Books

SHADOWMOUTH
by Meredith Oakes

ISBN: 9781840026795

BLACKBERRY TROUT FACE
by Laurence Wilson

ISBN: 9781849432436

DESERT BOY
by Mojisola Adebayo

from *Mojisola Adebayo: Plays One*

ISBN: 9781849430753

WHAT FATIMA DID...
by Atiha Sen Gupta

ISBN: 9781840029765

MRS REYNOLDS AND THE RUFFIAN
by Gary Owen

ISBN: 9781849430654

SHRADDHA
by Natasha Langridge

ISBN: 9781840029659

FIT
by Rikki Beadle-Blair

ISBN: 9781849430807

POSH
by Laura Wade

ISBN: 9781840029840

DNA
by Dennis Kelly

ISBN: 9781840028409

SPUR OF THE MOMENT
by Anya Reiss

ISBN: 9781840029857

THE LOSS OF ALL THINGS
by Chris Goode

from *Sixty-Six Books: 21st-Century Writers Speak to the King James Bible*

ISBN: 9781849432276

JAMES DEAN IS DEAD! (LONG LIVE JAMES DEAN)

from *Hollywood Legends: 'Live' on Stage*
by Jackie Skarvellis

ISBN: 9781840027693

KURT AND SID
by Roy Smiles
ISBN: 9781840029420

**LOVE STEALS US
FROM LONELINESS**
by Gary Owen
ISBN: 9781849430548

ONE MAN, TWO GUVNORS
by Richard Bean
ISBN: 9781849430296

THE DARK THINGS
by Ursula Rani Sarma
ISBN: 9781840029635

UNTITLED
by Inua Ellams
ISBN: 9781849431170

MIDDLETOWN
by Will Eno
ISBN: 9781849430661

OUR CLASS
by Tadeusz Slobodzianek /
Ryan Craig
ISBN: 9781840029468

IN THE PIPELINE
by Gary Owen
ISBN: 9781849430708

SHALOM BABY
by Rikki Beadle-Blair
ISBN: 9781849432139

CHEKHOV IN HELL
by Dan Rebellato
ISBN: 9781849431033

BEA
by Mick Gordon
ISBN: 9781849430067

**WE'RE GONNA MAKE
YOU WHOLE**
by Yasmine Van Wilt
ISBN: 9781849431316

LOWER NINTH
by Beau Willimon
ISBN: 9781849430364

BEARDY
by Tom Wells
from *Sixty-Six Books:
21st- Century Writers
Speak to the King James
Bible*
ISBN: 9781849432276

ZERO
by Chris O'Connell
ISBN: 9781840028812

THIS OTHER CITY
by Daragh Carville
ISBN: 9781849430494

UP ON ROOF
by Richard Bean
from *Bean: Plays Three*
ISBN: 9781840029130

BLUE HEART AFTERNOON
by Nigel Gearing
ISBN: 9781849431392

I HEART MATHS
by James Ley
from *The Ego Plays*
ISBN: 9781849432306

DEEP HEAT
by Robin Soans
ISBN: 9781849430906

THE MIRACLE MAN
by Douglas Maxwell
ISBN: 9781849430326

THE PROPHET
by Hassan Abdulrazzak
ISBN: 9781849434492

I AM THE WIND
by Jon Fosse /
Simon Stephens
ISBN: 9781849430715

THE RIOTS
by Gillian Slovo
ISBN: 9781849431996

THE KREUTZER SONATA
by Leo Tolstoy /
Nancy Harris
ISBN: 9781840029680

**SANCHO: AN ACT OF
REMEMBRANCE**
by Paterson Joseph
ISBN: 9781849431491

**BEHOLD THE COACH, IN A
BLAZER, UNINSURED**
by Will Eno
from *Oh, the Humanity
and other good intentions*
ISBN: 9781840028324

**DANDY IN THE
UNDERWORLD**
by Tim Fountain
ISBN: 9781849431149

BIRDSONG
by Sebastian Faulks/
Rachel Wagstaff
ISBN: 9781849430685

**LULLABIES OF
BROADMOOR:
WILDERNESS**
by Steve Hennessy
ISBN: 9781849431620

COLDER THAN HERE
by Laura Wade
ISBN: 9781840024715

RED
by John Logan
ISBN: 9781840029444

MUSWELL HILL
by Torben Betts
ISBN: 9781849431378

THE GODS WEEP
by Dennis Kelly
ISBN: 9781840029925

I, SHAKESPEARE
by Tim Crouch
ISBN: 9781849431262

**KALASHNIKOV: IN THE
WOODS BY THE LAKE**
by Fraser Grace
ISBN: 9781849432429

**OBEDIENTLY YOURS,
ORSON WELLES**
by Richard France
from *Hollywood Legends:
'Live' on Stage*
ISBN: 9781840027693

All the above books can be ordered from www.oberonbooks.com

by the same author

The Oberon Book of Modern Monologues for Men:
Volume One
9781840028256

The Oberon Book of Modern Monologues for Women:
Volume One
9781840028263

The Oberon Book of Modern Monologues for Women:
Volume Two
9781849434522

The Oberon Book of Modern Duologues
9781840028287

Classic Voice:
Working with Actors on Vocal Style
9781840028270

Modern Voice:
Working with Actors on Contemporary Text
9781849431712

WWW.OBERONBOOKS.COM

Follow us on www.twitter.com/@oberonbooks
& www.facebook.com/OberonBooksLondon

www.ingramcontent.com/pod-product-compliance
Ingram Content Group UK Ltd.
Pitfield, Milton Keynes, MK11 3LW, UK
UKHW020735280225
455688UK00012B/668